Theories of Health Justice

Theories of Health Justice

Just Enough Health

Thomas Schramme

ROWMAN &
LITTLEFIELD
INTERNATIONAL
London • New York

Published by Rowman & Littlefield International, Ltd.
6 Tinworth Street, London SE11 5AL
www.rowmaninternational.com

Rowman & Littlefield International, Ltd. is an affiliate of
Rowman & Littlefield
4501 Forbes Boulevard, Suite 200, Lanham, Maryland 20706, USA
With additional offices in Boulder, New York, Toronto (Canada), and London (UK)
www.rowman.com

British Library Cataloguing in Publication Information
A catalogue record for this book is available from the British Library

ISBN: HB 978-1-78660-143-8
ISBN: PB 978-1-78660-144-5

Library of Congress Cataloging-in-Publication Data Available

ISBN: 978-1-78660-143-8 (cloth : alk. paper)
ISBN: 978-1-78660-144-5 (pbk. : alk. paper)
ISBN: 978-1-78660-145-2 (electronic)

∞™ The paper used in this publication meets the minimum requirements of American National Standard for Information Sciences—Permanence of Paper for Printed Library Materials, ANSI/NISO Z39.48-1992.

Printed in the United States of America

Contents

Preface

For the longest time in human history, medicine and health care were services that people purchased out of their own pockets. Health was, therefore, up to a point, a consumer good. With the introduction of welfare-state institutions in many countries across the globe, health has become a good that requires collective efforts to be safeguarded and maintained; health risks have become collectivised. There are different systems in place to protect all citizens against those risks—funded by compulsory insurances or taxes—but the main purpose has been to disconnect ability to pay from access to medical treatment as well as to other types of health promotion. Today the value attached to individual and population health is very high. Accordingly, demand for the use of relevant institutions has constantly increased and caused higher costs than ever before. It is no wonder, then, that issues of justice in health care are high on the political agenda.

This book serves as an introduction to the main problems and theories of health justice. Social justice has traditionally been a topic discussed in political philosophy. Accordingly, this book is mainly concerned with philosophical theories. But it is not meant to be a study for philosophers only. Health justice is a problem that is of interest to every citizen and I have therefore aimed at a general readership by avoiding technical terms as much as possible and leaving out scholarly references. The interested specialist reader is referred to the section on further reading.

In pursuing the purpose of introducing the topic of health justice, my main method was to 'sort out' issues and theories. I do not give very detailed description of theories; rather, I aim at supporting readers to get a good grasp of the subject area so that they can study further by themselves and put alternative theories in the right context. Hence, this book does not replace the study of primary literature. Readers will be prepared to understand and read other studies in the right way and with a critical mind. This aim is in line with my understanding of the role of philosophy as regards issues of public concern. Sometimes philosophers are loathed for their restrained attitude when asked to provide expert opinion on normative issues, such as health justice. After all, they seem to be the experts in this field, but they usually restrict their role to laying out possible arguments and leave the decision to the public. Some critics seem to think that philosophers therefore do not really contribute to the enhancement of collective decisions. After all, decisions are still left to the political realm after philosophers have had their say. But this is false. Philosophy enhances public debate and political decision by explaining, clarifying and sorting out bad arguments. In so doing, it lays the intellectual foundation for citizens to achieve reasoned beliefs, which is more than simply having opinions.

The second main purpose of this book is to make an original contribution to the still-emerging field of philosophical studies on health justice. I argue in favour of a sufficientarian account of health justice—a theory that aims at enough health for all. My argument is most visible in the final chapter. In the other chapters I have aimed at a neutral description of available arguments without taking a stance. In those rare cases where I deviate from a neutral position, I have made that explicit. Philosophical reasoning is always critical in the sense of testing the plausibility of beliefs. Hence some level of engagement is unavoidable, even when introducing a topic.

The book is perhaps unusual in that it contains two chapters that thoroughly deal with basic medical terms: the concepts of disease, illness and health. To my mind this is unavoidable when discussing health justice, because the concept of disease functions as a kind of gatekeeper in accessing publicly funded health-care resources and the concept of health states the aim of health-care institutions. If we do not understand what disease and health are, we will never achieve a solid theory of health justice. I believe that this connection of issues of health justice and conceptual issues in the philosophy of medicine has not been acknowledged as much as it should. As will be seen, these concepts are contested and not straightforward at all.

Another feature of this book is that it is not merely concerned with medicine and health care, as traditionally understood. It integrates considerations regarding public health. Individual health is not merely determined by access to hospitals, doctors and the like but also—and perhaps more importantly—by people's circumstances and lifestyles. To prevent diseases is an important task of welfare states, and this can be done by many other means than medical instruments. Access to clean air and water, basic understanding of nutritional effects of food as well as many other determinants of health all have some impact on the maintenance and promotion of health. The book is accordingly not merely concerned with health-care justice in a narrow sense but, rather, has a wider remit. It addresses health justice more generally.

Since I interpret *health care* in a broad sense, including public-health instruments, I use both expressions *health justice* and *health-care justice* synonymously.

Many colleagues and friends have influenced my thinking about health justice and have helped to improve my work on the topic. Over the years, there have been far too many to mention them all, so I will restrict myself to only mentioning a few: I would like to thank Anton Leist, who was the first philosopher to introduce me to the relevant topics in the philosophy of medicine and who had a long-lasting influence on my understanding of philosophy and its role in public debates. I have benefited from many interesting discussions with my former colleagues and friends Steve Edwards, Mike McNamee and Hugh Upton. Lennart Nordenfelt, Christopher Boorse and Peter Hucklenbroich have been intellectual mentors whose own work in the philosophy of medicine has been inspirational. Stefan Huster has been a close friend of mine and deeply influenced my thinking on social justice, health justice and public health.

Last but not least, Ben Davies read the whole manuscript and provided invaluable comments and corrections, for which I am exceptionally grateful.

I would like to dedicate this book to the memory of my late brother, Markus, who unfortunately never cared much about his health.

Acknowledgements

I have worked on philosophical issues of social justice and specifically health justice for more than a decade, and I have also published on topics in the philosophy of medicine for quite some time. This book might be seen as a summary of my long-standing research and thinking in this area. I have therefore taken the liberty to draw on material I have published elsewhere; it has been reprinted with permission.

Schramme, Thomas. 'The Normative Significance of Social Determinants of Health'. *Ramon Llull Journal of Applied Ethics* 9 (2018): 155–65.

———. 'Goals of Medicine', in *Handbook of the Philosophy of Medicine*. Edited by Thomas Schramme and Steven Edwards, 121–28. Dordrecht: Springer Netherlands, 2017.

———. 'Health as Notion in Public Health', in *Handbook of the Philosophy of Medicine*. Edited by Thomas Schramme and Steven Edwards, 975–84. Dordrecht: Springer Netherlands, 2017.

———. 'Setting Limits to Public Health Efforts and the Healthisation of Society', *Zeitschrift für menschenrechte* 9, no. 2 (2015): 50–68.

———. 'Disability (Not) as a Harmful Condition: The Received View Challenged', in *Disability and the Good Human Life*. Edited by Jerome E. Bickenbach, Franziska Felder and Barbara Schmitz, 72–92. New York: Cambridge University Press, 2014.

———. 'Disadvantage and Equal Opportunity in Education: A Noncomparative Perspective', *Social Philosophy and Policy* 31, no. 1 (Jan. 2014): 135–49.

———. '"I Hope that I Get Old before I Die": Ageing and the Concept of Disease', *Theoretical Medicine and Bioethics* 34, no. 3 (2013): 171–87.

———. 'On the Relationship between Political Philosophy and Empirical Sciences', *Analyse und Kritik* 30, no. 2 (2008): 613–26. http://www.analyse-und-kritik.net/Dateien/56c1c477cbd92_ak_schramme_2008.pdf.

———. 'The Significance of the Concept of Disease for Health Care Justice', *Theoretical Medicine and Bioethics* 28, no. 2 (2007): 121–35.

———. 'A Qualified Defence of a Naturalist Theory of Health', *Medicine, Health Care and Philosophy* 10, no. 1 (2007): 11–17.

Schramme, Thomas, and Mark Siebel. 'Need-Based Justice from the Perspective of Philosophy'. *Need-Based Distributional Justice: An Interdisciplinary Perspective*. Edited by Bernhard Kittel and Stefan Traub. Heidelberg: Springer (in press).

Chapter One

The Concept of Disease

The concept of disease works as a kind of gatekeeper to accessing publicly funded health-care resources. Disregarding some special cases, if people have a disease, they have a claim to use medical resources in virtue of this condition. The relevant individual claims might be rejected for certain reasons, and hence claims are not fully developed entitlements or rights. Some reasons for rejecting a claim might be, for instance, that the costs of treatment would be too high or that the person was responsible for her condition. We will look into these rationales in later sections of the book. Here it suffices to acknowledge the normative force of the presence of disease. It constitutes a claim to get medical support. It should therefore be obvious that the concept of disease is of utmost normative significance: By working as a gatekeeper, disease determines entry to publicly funded health-care institutions. The concept of disease is accordingly a fundamental notion in thinking about health justice. It will be the main topic of this chapter.

We can identify the gatekeeping function as the positive connection between disease and claims of health justice, since the presence of disease has normative force. There could also be a negative connection in that the absence of disease might undermine any claim to the use of medical resources. According to this viewpoint, when people have no disease, it is not justified for them to use (publicly funded) medical resources. Lawrie Reznek, a philosopher of medicine, powerfully describes both connections: 'Judging that some condition is a disease commits one to stamping it out. And judging that a condition is not a disease commits one to preventing its medical treatment'[1]. Again, we will return to the latter problem at a later stage of the argument and focus, for now, on the positive link.

The reason for the connection between disease and claims of justice is the fact that disease is usually harmful to the affected person; disease is bad and should be cured or at least alleviated. Since many people cannot afford to pay the medical bills themselves, there should be a publicly funded system of medical support. Many people would subscribe to such an argument. But the connection of disease and normative claims is a contingent one. It has a certain historical development and is also located in a cultural context. Not all societies see medicine as a part of the bundle of welfare-state institutions; not all societies believe that harm should be the basis of normative claims. They might, for instance, believe that the basis should rather be merit or social status. Still, it seems that all human beings usually suffer when they are ill and that they normally want to get rid of the condition. Hence, if a society does at all cater for alleviating ailments that cannot be alleviated without support by others—in other words, if a society at all cares about the welfare of all citizens in the same way—then a publicly funded system of medical support will be on the agenda. After all, medicine is the institution that traditionally caters for alleviating harms that come with disease.

THEORISING ABOUT DISEASE

But what conditions constitute instances of disease? We know of historical examples of alleged disease—for instance masturbation—that proved to be simply based on faulty theories and usually on strong political and moral interests. In modern times, we find more examples for turning conditions into diseases, especially in relation to the normal decline of biological functioning due to the ageing of human organisms. This pathologisation—interpreting bodily or mental conditions as pathologies—is referred to as *disease mongering* when it is pursued intentionally. If we consider the mentioned normative implication of the concept of disease and the relevant interests that come with it, most significantly of the pharmaceutical industry, such widespread attempts to an ever-expanding interpretation of the concept of disease do not come as a surprise.

Consider an analogy from another area of knowledge: Let's say a zoologist called Bethan alleges to have found a hitherto unknown mammal on a field trip in the jungle. She intends to name it after herself: The Bethan mouse. In this example, we know what we need to do in order to make good her claim, because we know the definition of *mammal*. If the Bethan mouse fits the criteria for a mammal and really is a specimen of a new type of species, then the zoologist acted rightly. In this example from zoology, the extension of the concept—in other words, our prevalent theory of what a mammal is—decides the case (given certain additional assumptions about the concept of a species and regarding species membership). What we would need in medicine is an analogous theory of what a disease is, which could allow us to prevent disease mongering and to decide contested cases of alleged disease. One of the main reasons why this is unlikely to happen in medicine, however, is the fact that *disease* is not a category like *mammal*. The criteria for deciding which animals are mammals are all based on factual and empirically verifiable features. These criteria are included in a definition of *mammal*, which—despite historical changes and challenges—is widely accepted in zoology. Criteria for determining whether a condition is a disease are not straightforward at all, and there is also no received theory to begin with. In fact, there are numerous interpretations of what disease is that are competing for authority.

The most important strategy to avoid interpretations of the concept of disease that are simply driven by specific interests is to have an open, neutral discussion about such different theories of disease. Theories of disease provide a definition of the term *disease*, or at least a definition can be deduced from their theoretical elements. These theories thereby determine, by using certain criteria, which conditions are diseases. Let's go back to the example of masturbation: On what basis do most people today deem it to not be a disease? Most likely on grounds of a theory of disease they endorse, even if only implicitly. For instance, people tend to not believe that disease is simply due to persistent behavioural patterns. Most people would assume that such behaviour must be based on compulsion or lack of control. In addition, far fewer people today have the belief in an allegedly proper use of sexual organs; medical concepts are usually not seen as being determined by religious beliefs either. These are more negative reasons against seeing a specific condition or behavioural pattern as an instance of disease. In the end, we need to make explicit our reasoning by providing a theory of disease. This would include, most basically, a definition of the concept of disease with explicit criteria, which we can use to argue whether a specific condition falls under the concept. So the problem of deciding whether putative diseases are 'real' diseases has pushed us back to the level of theorising about disease. This raises concerns about the assessment and comparison of different theories of disease.

Let's have a look at such a theory: 'Individuals have a malady if and only if they have a condition, other than their rational beliefs or desires, such that they are incurring, or are at a significantly increased risk of incurring, a harm or evil (death, pain, disability, loss of freedom, or loss of pleasure) in the absence of a distinct sustaining cause'[2]. The first thing to note here is that the authors do not define the term *disease* but *malady*. The latter is a more old-fashioned term, arguably covering a broader area than the concept of disease, which seems to be restricted to the context of medicine. This difference will raise important questions regarding medical terminology later in this chapter. After all, we have numerous words to refer to medical ailments: *disease*, *illness*, *sickness*, *malady*, *disorder*, *pathology*. For the time being we can disregard their differences, as our focus is on defining medical terminology as an explicit foundation against which putative pathological conditions are checked.

According to Danner Clouser, Bernard Gert and Charles Culver, the authors just cited, masturbation is not a malady. It does not incur any of the harms or evils mentioned in the list. More importantly, their theory can be used to check any condition that is put forward as a medical condition. This is an extremely important function of such a definition. It helps us to make explicit the reasons for seeing a condition as a disease or not. It can help us avoid disease mongering because we can always critically discuss whether the features for seeing a condition—say, irritable bowel syndrome—as a medical condition are relevant on grounds of a theory of disease. Whether a definition really does exclude IBS is not the main issue here. Its main function is to enable a rational discussion about the status of putative medical conditions on the basis of explicit criteria.

There is still the issue of a multiplicity of theories of disease, though. How do we decide between them? When discussing the merits of different theories of medical concepts, we first of all weigh their clarity. After all, if we want to use such a theory to check suggested medical conditions, we want to gain some control over the direction of the process. Consider, for instance, the definition of *disease* by German medical theorist Karl Eduard Rothschuh, which he says is 'a state of subjective or clinical or social need for help due to a loss of the harmonious interaction of the physical, psychical or psychophysical parts of the body'[3]. It is not easy to say whether irritable bowel syndrome, or even masturbation, should count as a disease on the basis of this definition. To be sure, explanations as to what constitutes a loss of the harmonious interaction of the parts of the body is part of Rothschuh's theory of disease. Hence such a theory not only consists of a definition of *disease* but also contains further explanatory elements.

A second aspect of a good theory of medical terminology is its harmony with common assumptions about pathological conditions. This theory should exclude clear examples of nondisease and should include straightforward examples of pathological conditions. For instance, the theory put forward by Clouser and coauthors, it has been mentioned, would mean categorising pregnancy as a malady. This would seem to speak against the theory. Some readers might object that clearly pregnancy should qualify for access to publicly funded health-care resources. However, at this point we are concerned with the positive connection between *disease* and *claims of justice*. There might be grounds for granting access to health-care institutions other than disease—most importantly the prevention of disease. We will consider these later in the book.

All this implies that a theory of disease cannot simply be used to decide contentious disease labels once and for all. Such theories are themselves under scrutiny against certain assumptions concerning disease. We therefore need to appreciate a certain level of circularity, which cannot be avoided: assumptions about disease drive our assessment of theories, which are used to check our beliefs about disease. We aim at consistency in our beliefs and our verdicts about disease. This will be achieved by making explicit and critically discussing the reasons for assuming that any given condition is a disease or not. Without such a critical basis the important normative problem as to which conditions count as medically relevant and hence as forming an initial claim for using medical resources would be left to social and political tinkering without a firm foundation in rational debate. This is what makes theories of disease valuable.

Some theorists believe they can circumvent the problem of circularity by providing a descriptive theory of disease. They aim at describing the actual use of the concept of disease in medicine. After all, medical experts seem to be privy to the proper use of medical terminology. So why not build a theory of disease on common thinking in medicine and merely summarise in one coherent definition what has already been agreed upon? One problem with this is of course that such a consensus is far from visible in medicine. Experts disagree about many disease labels. A philosophically more important problem with this approach is that it does not allow for revisionary outcomes. In other words, a theory of disease should have some critical bite and allow us to challenge alleged cases of disease. This is especially pertinent in a situation where the concept of disease has become a kind of battlefield for pursuing economic and political interests.

The trajectory of our argument so far started from the normative implications of the concept of disease, which have led us to the need for theorising about disease. Otherwise we leave a problem of significant ethical and political relevance—namely, an issue of justice—to be decided by prevalent societal and political interests only. We want a rational basis for discussing issues of justice in health care. Theories of disease play an important part in fulfilling this task. Yet the multiplicity of theories of disease in the philosophy of medicine has pushed us to an even more abstract problem: how to decide between different theories of disease.

Whatever criteria of theory evaluation we come up with, we need to accept that theories of disease cannot only be ranked on the basis of how well they describe an alleged nature of disease. This would perhaps be different if disease were a phenomenon completely independent of human interests—if it were, as we put it in philosophy, a *natural kind*. But disease is not a natural kind. Take a theory of gold, for instance: the best theory of gold is the one that explains the nature of gold best, which relates to its chemical, structural and other intrinsic characteristics. The same aspects do not seem to apply to disease, though it will also be seen in this chapter that the fact that *disease* is not a natural-kind term should not lead us to believe that it therefore needs to be conceptualised on the basis of human interests only. There is certainly some 'reality' to disease that will be reflected in the best theories.

THEORIES OF DISEASE

There have been long-standing debates in philosophy of medicine about the causation and characteristics of disease. For instance, since antiquity numerous theorists have interpreted disease as a kind of imbalance. There were also important discussions about the ontological status of specific diseases, such as syphilis. Were diseases to be regarded as real entities that somehow invade the body or as theoretical abstractions? Similarly, it can be asked whether specific disease concepts can be discovered or should rather be considered to be human inventions and, hence, theoretical constructs. These are questions about the ontology of disease entities, about their mode of existence. These issues are not our concern here, despite their considerable importance in the history of medical theory. The question we raise is a conceptual problem: how to draw the boundaries between the phenomena of health and disease in a medical context. The main issue here is to determine a foundational medical norm, concerning the general concept of disease, not specific disease entities.

In the modern discussion within philosophy of medicine, roughly starting in the 1970s, the main bone of contention was whether the concept of disease is value-laden or descriptive. The respective theories were usually referred to as *normativism* and *naturalism*. It should be clear from what has been said so far that at least the first label might cause confusion, as the concept of disease states a norm, so in some respect every theory of disease would be normativist. Perhaps a better way to draw the distinction is by saying that one type of theory assumes values or value judgements to be an essential part of the definiens—the defining elements or criteria—of the concept of disease. A clear example of this understanding is put forward by H. Tristram Engelhardt Jr. who says that 'the concept of disease acts not only to describe and explain, but also to enjoin to action. It indicates a state of affairs as undesirable and to overcome. It is a normative concept; it says what ought not to be. As such, the concept incorporates criteria of evaluation, designating certain states of affairs as desirable and others as not so'[4]. Similarly, Rachel Cooper says that 'by "disease" we aim to pick out a variety of conditions that through being painful, disfiguring or disabling are of interest to us as people'[5]. The main aspect of the normativist type of theory is therefore that disease is a harmful condition. This allows for a straightforward explanation as to why masturbation is not a disease: it is not harmful, and no reasonable person considers it to be harmful.

Normativist theories need some additional elements to explain the specific nature of medical harms—as opposed to other human harms, such as envy and loneliness—or occasionally undesired bodily and mental traits and conditions, such as conjoined eyebrows, clumsiness or poor memory. Hence normativists usually allow for factual elements of determining medical conditions. They insist, however, that some amount of value judgement is necessary. According to this thinking, we cannot single out 'real' diseases by referring to facts alone.

A more extreme version of the normative perspective would be a kind of social constructivism, hence the claim that medical norms are purely based on cultural interpretation. Peter Sedgwick endorses this viewpoint, saying that, 'outside the significances that man voluntarily attaches to certain conditions, *there are no illnesses or diseases in nature*. . . . The fracture of a septuagenarian's femur has, within the world of nature, no more significance than the snapping of an autumn leaf from its twig: and the invasion of a human organism by cholera-germs carries with it no more the stamp of "illness" than does the souring of milk by other forms of bacteria'[6].

What should we make of such a claim? In one respect Sedgwick is, of course, right, if in a rather unexciting way. Surely nature itself does not contain medical categories; it does not impose any specific categories on us. We might as well call having brown hair or a high-pitched voice diseases—it would not be 'against nature'. But there are obviously good reasons why doing so would not really help us solve human problems dealing with harms that affect us. The very purpose of having a category *disease* in the first place needs to be considered here. I suppose humans introduced the concept to single out those conditions that impair their capacities in some respect and potentially require attention of specialists. These specialists are today called doctors, psychiatrists, nurses and medical personnel, more generally. Historically, apothecaries and other groups of people were dealing with diseases, too. So, altogether, despite Sedgwick's reasonable scepticism regarding the possibility of 'carving nature at its joints', there are certainly important reasons why we need the concept of disease. The focus should be on the criteria constituting a disease in relation to such theoretical and practical reasons. Even Sedgwick would probably agree.

In defending the usefulness of the concept of disease, we still encounter the problem of how exactly to conceptualise this category. Here we enter the debate between different theories of disease. Sedgwick clearly believes that nature cannot be our guide in putting forward criteria to determine which conditions are to be called diseases. However, this does not follow from the fact that categories, such as *disease*, are our own making. Human beings have studied organisms for a very long time and discovered numerous processes and conditions they can go through or be in. Scientists have good reasons to call some of these processes instances of *disease*. The concept of disease is introduced on the basis of certain human interests, but the criteria for disease themselves do not have to be evaluative; they can be purely factual. This is not unusual. Consider the criterion for the 'use-by' date for groceries, which defines the category of a legally sellable product in many countries. We could call groceries that are sold after the use-by date 'bad products' and consider them harmful to the consumer. Now surely it is a human invention to have such a category in the first place, and there is no 'nature' to follow here. Still, to determine which items belong in which category on the basis of the criterion is a purely factual problem; it simply requires checking the printed date against the actual date. More to our point here, it is convincing to hold that diseases are usually harmful to the affected person. It does not follow, however, that harmfulness is a relevant criterion of something being a disease. In other words, it is not straightforward that we need to make a value judgement when determining whether a specific condition is a disease or not. This is exactly what the naturalist theorists hold: they attempt to devise a value-neutral theory of disease.

The most influential and sophisticated theory in the naturalist camp has been developed by Christopher Boorse. He defines disease as 'a type of internal state which is either an impairment of normal functional ability, i.e., a reduction of one or more functional abilities below typical efficiency, or a limitation on functional ability caused by environmental agents'[7]. In Boorse's definition there are no criteria that involve evaluations in terms of disease being good or bad for the affected person. It nevertheless allows for an explanation as to why masturbation is not a disease: This is because such sexual practices do not involve an impairment of normal functioning ability.

Normal functional ability, according to Boorse's theory, is determined via biological and statistical findings regarding the makeup of organisms and the prevalence of certain traits. A theory of organismic functions can be based on the natural evolutionary history of relevant organisms or on assumptions regarding the biological goals of such organisms, most importantly individual survival. So there are varieties within the naturalist camp, but they agree that facts about the functioning of organisms determine the foundational medical norm.

A lot of ink has been spilled in relation to the question of whether Boorse's theory really is value-free, as he claims. For instance, some theorists have maintained that the concept of biological function, which has just been mentioned as an important element of his theory, cannot be defined without reference to values. Personally, I do not believe that this debate is helpful, because there are different ways a theory can be value-laden. Boorse's theory is not value-laden, if at all, in the same way that normativist theories are, since his theory does not imply welfare-related evaluations. We will see, in the next section, how the theoretical conflict between normativism and naturalism can even be explained in terms of a difference in perspectives. In other words, normativist and naturalist theories are compatible. They both attempt to conceptualise important, yet different, aspects of medical terminology.

A significant advantage of the naturalist over the normativist account, which is pertinent to our discussion about justice in health care, is the naturalist account's ability to restrict the prospects for political, industrial and societal interests to influence the boundaries of the concept of disease. This is mainly due to the fact that the naturalist account stays clear, as far as possible, from medically irrelevant reasons for expanding the extension of the concept of disease. It focuses on the scientific explanation of the processes and conditions, which do not function as they are supposed to or as they normally do.

It should be acknowledged that many further objections have been raised against naturalist theories and Boorse's specific version of it. We need to ignore these for the purposes of this book. There is one specific disadvantage of the naturalist perspective, however, that I would like to mention. Since the naturalist account sticks to the factual aspects of ill health, it cannot conclusively guide our decision making when considering issues of justice. Most importantly, at some point, especially when considering prioritisation or rationing of medical resources, societies want to make value judgements about the severity of disease, relative to other pathological conditions. A value-neutral account of disease cannot consider this element of a theory of healthcare justice. Accordingly, a naturalist theory of disease needs to be complemented by evaluative considerations. Still, it should be clear from what has been said so far that naturalism about disease can help provide a rational basis for medicine and keep expansive motives at bay.

DISEASE AND ILLNESS

It has already been acknowledged that not all theories of medical terminology talk about the same phenomena. Some theorists conceptualise *disease*, others *illness* and so on. These terms do not all have the same meaning. *Disease* is something a person has, a particular feature of an individual or even of a part of the organism, not a holistic description of the condition of the affected person altogether. We do not say that a person is diseased; but we can say that an organ is diseased. *Disease* is the umbrella term for those different conditions that are collated in medical classificatory systems, most importantly the *International Classification of Diseases* (ICD). *Illness*, in contrast, is a term that applies to a person. A person is ill; we do not usually say that a person has an illness, though it is not linguistically wrong. We certainly do not say that a person has, say, a liver illness or that their liver is ill.

To be sure, we should be careful not to read too much into such language use, though. Obviously our considerations are only based on one language among many: English. Other languages are not necessarily congruent with these linguistic characteristics. What is more, languages are flexible and historically malleable. We cannot expect language use to fully determine theories. Still, the mentioned differences help us to appreciate that there can be different perspectives on medical phenomena.

A useful way to capture one important difference in perspectives on medical phenomena is the distinction between disease and illness, which has just been introduced. It has also often been emphasised in the philosophy of medicine. *Disease* is usually seen as standing for the factual, general aspects of pathologies of specific processes in an organism. It contrasts with the notion of health. That is, if a person has a disease, she is not healthy, and vice versa. *Health*, in the medical context, usually is simply defined as 'the absence of disease'; it is meant to state a norm of bodily and mental functioning. We will return to the concept of health in the next chapter, as this is certainly not the only possible interpretation.

Disease is also usually seen as an absolute term that does not allow for grades. There are of course more severe diseases—say, cancer in contrast to a flu—but this does not mean that a person with cancer has more disease or is more diseased than someone with a flu. Disease as such does not have a specific degree. The impact will need to be assessed against criteria that involve value judgements—for instance, about levels of disability involved, impairment of well-being or economic consequences. These connections to evaluation are important, for instance, when making decisions about prioritising treatment of different diseases.

It is true that the kind of processes medicine acknowledges as underlying disease can be affected to different degrees. That means that organismic functioning can come in grades. Consider blood pressure: It is measured along a continuum, and there can be ample debate regarding the exact point at which high blood pressure becomes pathological. However, once a threshold and therefore a norm of health and disease has been established, some levels of blood pressure will be pathological and hence called *hypertension* at the upper threshold and *hypotension* at the lower threshold.

It should be acknowledged that actual medical nosology—that is, the theory and classification of diseases—does not always follow this pattern. Medicine knows of prepathological conditions, dispositions, risk factors and other conditions that undermine the neat distinction between healthy and pathological conditions. There are also terms in medical classification, such as *syndrome* or *disorder*, especially in psychiatry, that follow a different logic and do not live up to, as it were, the model of disease. We will return to this complication because it has some impact on the debate about justice in health care as well. Most importantly, we must ask whether disease dispositions support normative claims of the same strengths as the presence of disease.

At this point it suffices to conclude that the concept of disease can be understood as determining an absolute norm, focusing on the organism and its condition. A briefer way to put it is to say that *disease* is a theoretical notion, in the sense that it attempts to capture pathological processes and conditions without focusing on practical implications, such as a need to medically treat them. Personally I prefer to say that the concept of disease stands for a scientific perspective.

Illness, on the other hand, focuses on the nonfactual, welfare-related and personal elements of medical conditions. It puts forward what can be called an evaluative perspective. We would not, for instance, call someone ill whose well-being is not at all affected. As mentioned before, illness is a holistic feature, affecting the whole person, not merely a part of their body or mind. Importantly, there is hence an element of value judgement needed—mainly whether the condition is bad for the person—to establish the presence of an illness. At least potentially, this allows for two people in the very same condition to be either ill or not. For instance, a person who is colour-blind might be severely affected by her condition because she is an artist; she would regard the condition as an illness. Another person with the same visual condition—say, a farmer—might not be impaired in her well-being and hence not consider herself ill.

Illness is, according to this interpretation, not a general notion that applies to all people in the same way with a sufficiently similar organism. This feature puts the idea again in contrast to the concept of disease. *Illness* is, rather, an individual notion, which refers to a specific condition of a particular person, including more than just the internal elements of an organism. We will not find a medical textbook on illnesses or a classification of illnesses. Indeed, even the plural, *illnesses*, is only used in special cases. We should, however, not merely consider linguistic aspects, as mentioned before. For instance, the term *mental illness* is still in common use, though psychiatric nomenclature uses the term *mental disorder*, which lends itself more easily to generalisations. The main lessons to learn here are connected to the important differences between understanding disease and illness, not to language use.

If illness is connected to impairments in well-being, an important question follows: who is to judge whether a person is ill or not? This is especially pertinent if the presence of illness is the basis for claims to health-care resources. From what has been said so far about the concept of illness, one might think that the presence of illness is determined by the subjective assessment of the affected person alone. If she feels unwell, she has an illness; if not, she is not ill. But we can think of examples where people are oblivious to impairments of their welfare, and we could hence consider identifying illness in a person in contrast to her own evaluation. For instance, people in the manic phase of bipolar disorder feel fantastic and most likely would not consider themselves ill. So at least for the purposes of reasoning about health-care justice, it seems unhelpful to base claims on subjective assessments only.

Another contrast to the concept of disease that should be mentioned is that illness can come in grades. The very fact that the concept is linked to matters of the good human life and its impairments allows gradual thinking. After all, well-being and other conditions related to it, such as welfare or happiness, can all come in higher or lower degrees; so we can say that a person with cancer is more ill than someone who has the flu.

Interestingly, illness can be compatible with disease. We have already briefly seen, in the case of colour blindness, how this might be possible. There are many more examples, some of which have involved significant public debate. Deafness, for instance, does not necessarily impair the well-being of affected people, as many of them have repeatedly emphasised. But it would be hard to see how deafness could be considered medically normal. It certainly seems to be the case that auditory perception is a function of certain organs of the human organism and hence that dysfunctions in relation to it should be considered pathological. Still, it needs to be acknowledged that deafness does not necessarily undermine the well-being of a deaf person. In other words, deafness might not always be an illness. It is only possible to mark such differences if we recognise the mentioned distinction in perspectives; otherwise we talk past each other. If we conflate the presence of disease—that is, a factual statement about the condition of an organism—with the presence of illness—that is, an impairment of well-being—then we are prone to faulty value judgements.

A CONCEPTUAL FOUNDATION FOR JUSTIFYING CLAIMS IN HEALTH CARE?

We have just seen that there can be disease without illness; can there also be illness without disease? This is a question about the relation between the concepts. In other words, it is a question about conceptual priority. Within philosophy of medicine this problem has stirred up some amount of discussion. It is helpful, first of all, to get a grip on the idea of a conceptual priority. By this I mean that the extension of one concept is restricted by the other: Naturalists believe that in order to qualify as an illness at all, a condition would have to be deemed a disease. In contrast, if theorists believe that *illness* is conceptually prior, they would allow for medical conditions that are not necessarily instances of disease.

Some theorists claim that the concept of illness is prior because illness is the starting point of medical concern. People go to doctors and possibly learn about disease only if they have a complaint. However, this is irrelevant. As explained, the issue under discussion is about a conceptual relationship. The fact that we first know about illness and then disease does not make any difference in terms of the logical relation of the concepts. If theorists nevertheless want to insist on this particular priority of illness, they can call it epistemologically prior. But it does not solve the problem posed here. The issue concerns the extensions of the two concepts and how they are related.

When putting the issue of conceptual priority into the context of health-care justice and the starting point of this chapter—namely, the normative consequences of using medical terminology—then it might be easier to see why there are strong reasons to deem the concept of disease as conceptually prior. The main reason is the fact that the concept of disease can help to build a firm and objective foundation for normative claims. Surely most societies would not want to leave the decision about which conditions deserve publicly funded treatment to subjective evaluation. The latter is strongly connected to the concept of illness, though it should be said that there might be theories of illness that would allow for objective value judgements in relation to medical conditions. For instance, the theory mentioned earlier, by Clouser, Gert and Culver, lists objective harms. So perhaps it is not so much the logical relation between concepts that counts but the reasons given for justifying the extension of foundational medical terminology. These reasons should be nonarbitrary, scientifically valid and, as much as possible, objective.

According to the argument we have explored so far, claims of health justice would be based on facts about a condition—briefly, whether it is a disease. This would help exclude unjustified claims. However, the conceptual foundation does not lead by itself to a sufficient basis of a theory of health justice, because justified claims as such do not form entitlements. This is because not every disease will be severe enough to justify the use of scarce resources. In addition, scarcity of resources might require comparative assessments regarding the relative severity of different disease types. In other words, prioritising the use of medical resources leads us to complex evaluations that cannot be done by conceptual clarification. But then, someone might say, if it is the case that we need an evaluative perspective anyway when devising a full-fledged theory of justice in health care, why not go straight to an evaluative foundation? For instance, we could introduce a term of art, such as 'socially accepted medical condition', that would serve as an umbrella term for entitlements to use medical resources.

It should not come as a surprise that I would oppose such an approach. The reason is that, first, we would sever a historically strong connection between the presence of disease and claims to use medical resources, and, second, we would unnecessarily ignore an important source of reasons for justifying claims of justice—namely the objective perspective on conditions of human organisms. To be sure, there might be good reasons to additionally offer publicly funded medical treatment for conditions that are not diseases. Perhaps the best examples in this respect are services that help alleviate possible severe harm and at the same time can most effectively be treated by medicine. However, it would always be clearly visible that these additional claims are not based straightforwardly on the fact that a disease is present. The normative reasons given for the use of medical resources in case of nondisease would have to be strong and of a special kind. In contrast, the traditional reason that a disease is present leads straightforwardly to a widely accepted claim to the use of socially provided health-care resources.

CONCLUSION

This chapter has focused on philosophical theories of disease. The concept of disease bears significance for a theory of health justice, because to have a disease traditionally justifies an initial claim to the use of publicly funded health-care resources. That is why theories of health justice should be informed by ongoing discussions in the philosophy of medicine. Disease, however, is a contested concept; it does not have 'natural' boundaries or an accepted definition. Still, it was argued in this chapter that the concept of disease can be based on a scientific foundation. It does not have to be seen as determined merely by human interests.

The main contenders in the philosophical debate are called naturalism and normativism. Despite some overlap, these theories put forward different perspectives on ill health. Naturalism considers conditions and processes of organisms, ignoring what these might mean for human beings; it usually sees biological dysfunction of organisms as an essential criterion of pathological conditions. Normativism, on the other hand, considers ill health essentially as impairment of well-being of a specific, medical kind. I have argued that naturalism and normativism are compatible, as they address different perspectives that can be conceptually distinguished by differentiating between *disease* and *illness*.

Finally, we have examined whether there might be a conceptual priority between *disease* and *illness*. I have argued that especially for the purposes of a theory of health justice it would be important to acknowledge *disease* as conceptually prior, because it allows for the restriction of problematic expansions of claims to the use of publicly funded resources. The concept of illness is still of significance, though, because *disease* does not carry any direct link to human well-being. A theory of health justice would normally focus on those diseases that are bad for human beings. Accordingly, the perspective of normativism is also required.

Chapter Two

Health

In the previous chapter we discussed the concept of disease as a gatekeeper for accessing publicly funded health care. This chapter will focus on health. We will see that health is not simply the opposite of disease, as *health* allows for different interpretations. Our first task will therefore be to distinguish different accounts of health. Health can be seen as one of the primary goals of medicine. It sets the target when using medical resources. This has implications for issues of justice: Disease only determines the just cause, as it were, of medical intervention. The aim of health at least partly determines the amount and type of medical resources needed as a matter of justice. For instance, curing a broken bone usually requires painkillers, a cast, rest and physiotherapy but not spending a day in an oxygen tent or getting a full-body massage. However, as we will see, the exact details of what is indicated as treatment in a particular case and what is a fully justified claim to the use of medical resources is not only determined by these medical aspects but also by social and political concerns.

In addition, health understood as more than the absence of disease allows for further potential claims of justice. Even so-called enhancements might form valid claims of justice. Someone might, for instance, claim that she is not fully healthy if she does not get treatment for a feature of her body she despises. To assess such potential claims of justice requires an account of the normative significance of health. Our second task in this chapter will therefore be to discuss the value of health in its various interpretations.

Like many other normative quarrels we can identify in societies, the debate about justice in health care is partly based on conceptual confusion. As argued in the previous chapter, claims of justice in the context of medicine usually start from the presence of disease. Disease normally poses a kind of harm to people, and health care is a common means to tackling this kind of harm. Since disease is a kind of ill health, it seems straightforward to focus on health and its restrictions when thinking about health-care justice. However, this move—shifting the focus from disease to the restrictions of health—comes with conceptual implications that easily lead to confusion. This is because some interpretations of the notion of health allow for ill health to be present in case of conditions that do not qualify as disease. Consider the definition of the World Health Organization: 'Health is a state of complete physical, mental and social well-being and not merely the absence of disease and infirmity'[1]. According to this understanding, a person who is unhappy with the shape of her nose is not in a state of health, although an undesired shape of a nose is not normally regarded a disease. Now, if we add that the aim of medicine is health and that just claims are based on lack of health, then we have a template for justifying claims of justice that go way beyond the mentioned cause of treating disease.

The way forward here is to get a better grasp of the concept of health. There seems something wrong with the WHO's definition. But it also seems to be onto something, as health indeed seems to be a kind of ideal, to be understood in its own right, not merely in some 'absence of disease'. So the first point to make is that we can understand the concept of health as an ideal or as a minimum. The distinction is sometimes described, perhaps a bit confusingly, in terms of a positive in contrast to a negative account of health.

POSITIVE VERSUS NEGATIVE CONCEPTIONS OF HEALTH

Many people would probably agree that it is important to get a grasp of the concept of health in its own right and not simply in terms of the absence of disease. But the idea of understanding health as a positive notion is itself ambiguous. We may either intend a direct definition of the term. *Health*, according to this interpretation, should not be defined in negative terms, as the absence of something, but in its own specific description. Alternatively, someone might aim at a positive conception of health—that is, at a definition that explicates an ideal and not just a bare minimum. Here the term *health* is understood as demanding more than merely the absence of disease to apply. Health, in this quest for a positive conception, becomes an ideal. The WHO's definition states both a positive definition and a positive conception of health: it defines *health* in positive terms, and it demands more for health to be present than simply for disease to be absent.

The far more important aspect for normative purposes is the notion of health as an ideal. In fact, even the ideal conception of health in the WHO's interpretation can be transferred into a negative definition: 'Health is merely the absence of disease and infirmity. Disease and infirmity are states where complete physical, mental and social well-being is lacking'. The upshot of the discussion so far about positive conceptions of health is that the substance of the definitions of medical terminology is decisive, not the formal aspects of their definition—that is, whether it is defined as an absence of something or in direct terms.

Many scholars have criticised the WHO definition of health for confusing health with an ideal state of happiness. Clearly happiness—understood as the best possible state of well-being—is not a straightforward aim of medicine; or, perhaps even more clearly, happiness is not a reasonable aim of publicly funded health care. It would actually open the floodgate to all kinds of unwarranted claims if we would ground debates about justice in health care on the WHO definition. For instance, envying one's neighbour's car, which comes with a lack of complete physical, mental and social well-being, would potentially lead to a claim of justice due to ill health. Yet, as mentioned before, the WHO definition nevertheless seems to be onto something—and, of course, it should be added that it was never introduced as an element of a theory of health justice. It mainly served political aims of including aspects of well-being in devising health-care institutions and expanding a restricted medical focus to social aspects.

Perhaps a better way to honour positive aspects of health, over and above the absence of disease, would be to avoid stating an impossible ideal. A theory of health should not lose the connection to the goals of medicine and especially to the normative consequences of using medical terminology. This would allow us to restrict claims of justice, similar to the negative conception of health as absence of disease. But it would also allow us to acknowledge the connection of medicine and welfare.

Probably the best account of health based on such a positive conception was developed by the philosopher Lennart Nordenfelt. His definition of health reads, 'A is healthy if, and only if, A has the ability, given standard circumstances, to realize his vital goals, i.e. the set of goals which are necessary and jointly sufficient for his minimal happiness'[2].

The first part of Nordenfelt's account might seem an unfeasible conception of health, similar to the WHO definition, because it includes the criterion of individual goals, which may be quite far-reaching. But he adds a restriction: vital goals are aspirations whose realisation is necessary and jointly sufficient for minimal happiness. Hence, to be considered healthy one need not have the ability to realise all the goals one happens to have. Good health does not imply having the ability to achieve complete happiness. Nordenfelt's definition of health is less expansive than the WHO's.

But one might still want to argue that this definition is too broad, since it seems to cover certain inabilities, which should not count as instances of ill health after all. Consider Lily, an athlete, who struggles, for her whole adult life so far, to become an accomplished high jumper but does not succeed. Let us establish that her ambition is to vault over two meters, but she is unable to carry out the task. We may agree that succeeding in this effort is one of Lily's vital goals, because to not succeed means that she is not only minimally happy but actually frustrated and distraught. She is unable to realise at least one of her vital goals, and therefore she is not healthy, according to Nordenfelt's definition.

It seems, however, that we would only deem Lily unhealthy or in a state of ill health if she suffers from a disease. Indeed, the reason why we would regard any condition to be a disease seems to be entirely independent of an individual's ambitions. But Nordenfelt apparently needs to state that Lily is in ill health, because she is unable to realise all of her vital goals. This has a further awkward implication: Lily can become healthy by changing her goals. If her ambitions were more modest, her disability to cross the two-meter bar would not affect her vital goals, and hence she would be healthy.

We have now reached a very basic clash of interpretations regarding the concept of health: a more narrow medical interpretation, where health is a minimum of normal organismic functioning, and a more welfare-oriented interpretation, which sees health on a scale that allows for different grades. Ill health, according to this second interpretation, is not restricted to the presence of disease.

It therefore seems that the kind of objection raised here against Nordenfelt's conception only makes sense on the basis of a strictly medical interpretation of health. According to this view, health and ill health are opposites. It then seems strange to deem Lily to be in what we would call a 'medical condition' on the basis of her high ambitions. However, Nordenfelt's theory of health simply is not a medical theory, in the narrow sense of the term, but a welfare theory of health. It analyses health in terms of human abilities and their relation to happiness. According to this theory, health comes on a continuum; it allows for grades of health. As explained in the previous chapter, this is impossible, or at least not possible in the same way, in theories of health that interpret health as a minimum—that is, as an absence of disease.

There is nothing wrong with welfare theories of health. However, they might lead to confusion, because bad health is usually regarded as a medical problem. As regards a theory of health justice, welfare theories of health might lead to numerous claims that seem unsubstantiated. Still, such theories point at an important element: the fact that health is connected to human well-being. For purposes of health justice, it will be important to discuss thresholds of enough health to avoid unrestricted claims of justice along the continuum of more and better health.

HEALTH AS WELL-BEING

Perhaps the strongest reason why health is seen as an important element of social justice is the fact that ill health regularly comes with impairments of well-being. Illness is harmful; for instance, it involves pain or incapability. Not being healthy, in other words, is usually intrinsically bad for the affected person; but we have already acknowledged in the first chapter that not all instances of disease affect well-being. We will see, in the next section, that impairments of health can also be instrumentally disadvantageous, hence adding instrumental harm as well. Still, harmful conditions, especially if they are due to brute bad luck, pose immediately convincing scenarios for considerations of social justice.

To make people as happy as possible or to always improve their well-being is, in contrast, not normally seen as a matter of social justice—at least, not by real institutions of welfare states. Rather, it is the aim of preventing, removing or compensating harm that raises concerns of justice. Hence, the direct focus of theories of health justice is the contrastive condition to health: disease or illness. As we have seen, not all impairments in ideal health are harmful.

So, why discuss health at all in its own right in a theory of health justice? Why not focus instead on disease? At the beginning of this chapter, the main reason for focussing on health in its own right was mentioned: whereas disease is the cause of medical intervention, health is its aim. The latter is not always achieved in virtue of eliminating disease. So, we need to come to grips with the notion of health. If we consider health to be a welfare notion, as introduced in the previous section, then it seems fairly obvious that disease can actually go along with individual health. On a cursory look, the assumption of such a compatibility of disease and health seems contradictory. But consider the case of, say, coeliac disease—a condition affecting the digestive system and involving adverse immune reaction to gluten, a protein common in many foods and some drinks. Depending partly on the severity of the specific case, coeliac disease might not involve a significant impairment in well-being. According to Nordenfelt's welfare theory introduced above, it is certainly imaginable that a person with coeliac can realise her vital goals. Hence health—understood as welfare condition—and disease are compatible in this individual case.

There might also be more general examples of diseases that are compatible with health. Some diseases, despite being pathological, might not give rise to impairments of well-being, either because they are minor or because affected people can easily adapt to the condition. This is important for a theory of health-care justice, because it provides a reason to doubt that certain conditions, despite being pathological, justify claims of justice. For instance, hardly anyone would deem that a mild sunburn justifies claims of justice, despite its being a pathological condition of the skin. Severe forms of sunburn might of course be quite harmful and indeed call for treatment. Hence, to justify related claims of justice there will always need to be some kind of evaluation of pathological conditions in terms of well-being.

Perhaps more importantly, the concept of health not only modulates just causes of health care but also steers claims to specific resources. This is because claims to medical resources will focus on the means required to get back to health. Getting back to health does not always imply getting rid of disease. After all, *health* denotes, according to the welfare conception, being in a state of sufficient well-being. Getting back to health might require the provision of compensatory means to balance the harm of illness. We can call this process 'healing', because patients are made 'whole' again in terms of well-being. The notion of healing can be contrasted with curing disease. The latter is not always a possible or necessary way back to well-being. Hence, the aim of health can modulate the claims to the means of treatment. In health-care practice this judgement about required means is captured in the notion of medical indication. Indicated treatment refers to the required resources to bring a person back to health, understood in terms of well-being.

To illustrate both aspects—the notion of health modulating claims as such and modulating required resources to meet claims—let's consider the example of in vitro fertilisation, or IVF, which has stirred up considerable debate in many countries. It seems obvious that infertility is a pathological condition, hence giving rise to an initially justified claim to the use of socially secured health-care resources. However, in situations where the medical condition itself cannot be cured, we need to consider what the indicated treatment is, if any. Such an assessment is surely not a purely medical task but involves value judgements in relation to human well-being. In the case of infertility, there is an available compensatory technique allowing procreation by artificial means. IVF, if successful, can achieve health in the sense of ensuring the aim of using reproductive organs: to conceive children. However, the harm of not having children can be met by other than medical means, most importantly by adoption. Therefore, it would need to be discussed whether being unable to have genetically related children is a harm that needs to be compensated. Here we need to determine what *health* in relation to reproduction exactly implies. Further, it is not clear how many numbers of IVF cycles would need to be offered. In other words, even if it were assumed that IVF is an indicated means to tackle the medical condition of infertility, it is not straightforward whether a chance or the actual realisation of such compensation has to be offered as a matter of justice. Again, such debates involve considerable value judgements, which are of course informed by scientific findings regarding the risks, costs and benefits of IVF.

In summary, so far we have considered the need for a focus on health in addition to the notion of disease. The latter was the focus of the previous chapter; it sets the boundaries for just causes of claims to health care. In other words, the presence of disease is a rightful occasion for putting forward a claim for health-care justice. Health is an important additional focus because it sets the aim of medical intervention. Health as medical normality—as absence of disease—is not always a feasible or desired goal of medical intervention. Health as minimal well-being, as absence of harm due to pathology, sets the target. We can express this by saying that curing disease is not the only way back to health. Rather, healing the person is the proper aim. This implies that the idea of health, interpreted as a welfare notion, modulates claims of justice based on the presence of disease. It might do so by undermining the assumption of the harmfulness of disease. More importantly, the aim of health might also at least partly determine the type and amount of required resources for a medical intervention. We call the process of determining these resources medical indication. The modulation of claims due to the notion of health is illustrated in the IVF example.

Health as well-being is a notion that might be restricted by a threshold. It does not imply perfect welfare but a minimal amount of well-being. This idea obviously requires more analysis. We will return to it when discussing the concept of need and the theory of sufficientarianism later in the book. In Nordenfelt's approach, health has been fleshed out in terms of the capacity to fulfil one's vital goals, where these are defined as necessary and together sufficient for minimal individual happiness. So, despite using a gradual and indeed ideal metric—namely, well-being—not all welfare theories of health need to be unlimited in supporting claims of justice.

HEALTH AS AN ASSET

We have just seen that health can be seen as intrinsically valuable. Being healthy is good for human beings simply because it implies being in an unharmed condition. Health can also be deemed instrumentally valuable: when we are healthy we are able to do things we care about. Health, according to this interpretation, is a means to other ends. In other words, health is here construed as an asset for people. It helps people pursue opportunities.

Similarly to health as well-being, health as an asset comes in grades. There are different levels of health a person might enjoy. How healthy a person really is depends on how well the relevant mental and physical condition enables her to reach her goals. For example, when a cook has a dysfunction of her taste buds—say, due to a cold—she is not healthy. She would be even less healthy were she to lose her sense of taste completely. An academic with a cold who is working on a book might not be affected by this same medical condition and hence not be deemed to be in a state of ill health at all. Perhaps it is worth reminding the reader at this point that such a gradual account of health is in contrast to the negative definition of health, where a person is either healthy or not. As has been said before, it is important to keep different accounts separate. Medically speaking, both the cook and the academic with a cold have a disease and are hence in ill health.

Understanding health as an asset potentially opens up scope for considerations over and above the absence of disease. Instruments can always be improved, up to the point of perfection. Similarly, biological functions can be more or less effective or efficient to realise certain goals. For instance, a person working night shifts might deem the capacity to cope with lack of sleep an asset. Hence, improving this capacity would make her healthier, although having difficulties with sleep deprivation is not a disease. So, even levels of normal biological functioning, which would be medically normal according to the naturalist reading, can be worse than others and hence deemed less healthy, according to the asset reading.

It is important to notice that when we interpret health as an asset we also automatically include alternative conditions in the assessment of individual health, including possibly other people's conditions. This might sound odd: how should the level of health of a person be affected by the health conditions of others? The very term *asset* will hopefully help us understand the relationship to health, because it is an economic term and we are here considering situations where people need health as a means to reach goals. How effective and efficient they are in reaching their goals depends on the level of their mental and physical fitness and on the level of health of others—at least in competitive scenarios. Consider competing in a race: whether or not a runner has a chance to win is not only determined by her own level of fitness but also by her opponents' health condition. Obviously, with this interpretation of health we have found a reading congenial to a very influential idea in theories of justice, especially egalitarian thinking: fair equality of opportunities seems very strongly connected to health. Similarly, the idea of a level playing field seems to require equal individual levels of health.

We can expand this idea of health as an asset across the whole life span. Good health can give people more or better opportunities to pursue life plans, to live to a normal life span, and indeed it provides the very capabilities to plan one's life and develop one's ideas of how to live. Hence our level of health over time has a foundational impact on how well people's lives go. The current interpretation also shows the ubiquitous value of health, as it is beneficial in almost all contexts of life. Norman Daniels, for instance, a very influential theorist of health-care justice, succinctly describes, along with his coauthors, the value of health: 'By keeping people close to normal functioning, health care preserves for people the ability to participate in political, social and economic life. It sustains them as fully participating citizens, as "normal competitors" in all spheres of social life'[3].

Similarly to the case of impairments in well-being, we can immediately appreciate the normative significance of ill health when we follow this interpretation. However, it should be noted that the harm suffered because of disease according to this account is at least partly comparative: We might be *less* able to live a life according to our own plan than are others due to ill health; or we might have *reduced* chances to compete in different spheres of life, but this is a different kind of harm than the one suffered by enduring pain or by incapability. I will call this kind of comparative harm 'disadvantage'. Hence, impairments of health, which is understood as an asset, pose disadvantages. This puts the kind of harm due to ill health in contrast to the harm suffered according to the account that interprets health as well-being: In one interpretation disease is comparatively bad for the affected person—she is in a worse condition than in alternative possible conditions. According to the other interpretation, impairments of health are noncomparatively bad; they are harmful in their own right. We will later see that these two readings lead to different claims of justice.

Can there be a threshold of enough health within the asset account of health similar to the notion of minimal happiness we found in Nordenfelt's welfare theory? Such a threshold seems difficult to set, because at least competitive scenarios always allow for better or worse chances of individual people to compete. In terms of the asset theory of health, this would mean that there are always comparatively worse levels of health in some people. Nevertheless, it should be possible to determine levels of good-enough chances—for instance, when considering the opportunities to live a decent life. Daniels, for instance, just mentioned, actually restricts his theory of health-care justice to medical conditions, which are deemed unhealthy according to the standard of health understood as absence of disease. Only diseases allow for claims of health justice, not disadvantages that are due to other causes. 'Impairments of normal species functioning reduce the range of exercisable opportunities open to individuals from which they may construct their "plans of life" or "conceptions of the good"'[4]. According to Daniels's account, not every comparatively worse level of fitness grounds claims of health-care justice, but only pathological conditions, which are by definition worse conditions than conditions that fulfil the medical norm of health. In other words, Daniels allows for a threshold of enough health due to his minimal definition of health as absence of disease.

Other theories of health that put health in the perspective of competitive scenarios will lead to more far-reaching claims of health justice. If health allows for grades without limits, there will always be some people who are less healthy and hence disadvantaged through no fault of their own. Being disadvantaged through no fault of one's own is the main reason for claims of justice from the perspective of equality of opportunity. Hence, from an unlimited account of health follow unlimited claims to health-care resources, because these will enhance the chances of some and level the playing field for all. We will now examine how such a perspective of health as an asset pans out if the determinants of health are included as well. This is done in public health.

HEALTH IN PUBLIC HEALTH

Many societies are not only concerned directly with the health of individuals; states also focus on preventing disease through measures such as provision of clean water, containment of contagious diseases and screening programmes to identify genetic dispositions. In addition, the idea of health promotion has gained more attention. The improvement of health conditions, especially for vulnerable and disadvantaged groups, has become a major political concern on a global scale. Public health is the theory and practice of fulfilling this societal task of protecting the health of the population. From a philosophical perspective it is important to ask what *health* means in public health. This issue is rarely discussed, maybe because it is thought to have a straightforward answer. But it will be seen that, on the contrary, the notion of health in public health is far from clear.

A first issue concerns whether health is understood as a negative or positive concept—that is, as explained above, whether it is interpreted as the absence of disease or as something over and above such a minimal understanding. Public health indeed seems to include both these aspects, as can be seen in two definitions of public health. The first focuses on the negative aspects: 'Public health is the prevention of disease and premature death through organized community effort'[5]. The second definition states that public health is 'the science and art of preventing disease, prolonging life and promoting health through organised efforts of society'[6]. In this definition the idea of health promotion is explicitly mentioned. It allows for a possible expansion of the concept of health over and above the absence of disease.

A second issue concerns the emphasis of public health on the social determinants of health. It has been an important finding that the health status of individuals not only depends on their internal condition, such as the well-functioning of their organs, but also, and maybe more importantly, on their living conditions. This was first mainly seen in relation to the physical environment—for instance, in regard to hygienic conditions or housing. Over the last decades, the social determinants of health have been acknowledged to extend to far more factors, including working conditions, social relationships and public safety. These more remote 'causes of the causes', however, pose a theoretical problem, because being at (increased) risk of falling ill—for instance, because of a stressful and oppressive work atmosphere—is not the same as being in ill health. Conceptually, there is an important distinction between a particular health disposition and a healthy status. We have already seen that this distinction is related to the significant difference between a comparative and an absolute understanding of health. In focusing on healthy circumstances, public health is prone to confuse health dispositions and health statuses.

Third, public health is not only concerned with the health of individual citizens but also with the health of populations. This raises conceptual issues concerning the object to which a certain health status is ascribed. Is it the aggregate sum of individuals in a particular population that makes up the group's health status, or is a population deemed to be an entity in its own right that can also have a particular health status? To ascribe a certain level of health to populations raises not only ontological questions concerning individualism versus collectivism but also practical problems of measurement.

Finally, the very fact that public health is not just a science but a practice aiming at a common good makes the concept of health in public health in a distinctive way a normative notion. Health is here obviously understood as a good that should be protected and promoted. Indeed, it is usually seen as a moral concern if populations within a society, or globally, have different health statuses not due to their own choices but because of the social conditions they are living in. The conceptual problem here is one of a potential confusion between a scientific, and possible value-neutral, account of health in contrast to an interpretation of health in terms of political interests.

Usually public health experts focus on particular socioeconomic groups—for instance, unemployed persons or single mothers. When epidemiologists refer to population health, they usually mean the statistically aggregated sum of individual health traits or health statuses. The aggregation that leads to an account of population health depends on certain summary measures. Alternatively, but maybe more controversially, population health might be seen as a distinctive category, more than just the aggregate of individual health statuses.

The particular way groups or populations are determined depends on the purpose of a study. Ultimately, considerations in public health rely on hypotheses about social or socioeconomic determinants of health. Hence, epidemiologists aim at findings about possible correlations between particular circumstantial aspects of citizens and their health conditions. In this respect, the population perspective is instrumental to understanding causes of individual disease that are of a social nature.

Findings may be sought regarding socioeconomic aspects, such as income, educational background or gender, or behavioural aspects, such as lifestyle and diet. With these statistical correlations it is possible to make comparisons between populations regarding their health, even on an international level. Obviously it is also possible to compare different policies in tackling possible inequalities. In more popular publications, public-health scholars then end up with simple slogans, such as 'inequality is bad for your health', which only make sense from a population perspective. Such a collective perspective, though, it needs to be stressed, tends to ignore aspects on the individual level—for instance, individual responsibility for health status.

As we have seen, the fact that public health allows for grades of health opens the possibility to discuss health promotion in a way that includes enhancing health over and above the absence of disease. This is exactly the area where the worries about 'healthism' begin. Health, understood in a positive sense, as in the WHO definition, does not have an internal normative stoppage point or threshold of adequate health. More health is always better than less. For egalitarians in the debate on health justice, more health might also be required for some groups as a matter of justice because they are in worse health than other populations due to factors for which they are not responsible. What is more, according to the public-health perspective improvement of health is not merely, and maybe not even primarily, a matter of improving the internal resources of a person, such as stamina and nutrition, but also of the social determinants of health, such as quality of work environment, access to leisurely activities and so on. We can accordingly think of many ways to—if only indirectly—improve health dispositions of citizens by improving their environment as well as changing their lifestyles. Hence the possible scope for public-health interventions is very wide to say the least. One way to avoid these problems would be to introduce a threshold of 'enough' health, hence a sufficient grade of health that every citizen should be able to reach, without overreaching the target of adequate health promotion. But it is far from trivial to determine and justify such a threshold.

Another way forward is to explicitly acknowledge the political dimension of the notion of health in public health. After all, health here is not simply a scientific notion. It is rather what might be called a *functional notion*, as its content is driven by public concerns about what we, as a political community, want to publicly secure for every citizen. What citizens in a particular society regard as sufficient health within public health is therefore also influenced by theories and beliefs regarding social justice.

The health of the population is a common good. It is a public task to secure it. But it is not determined by the notion of health itself up to which level it ought to be safeguarded. This depends on issues that go far beyond conceptual issues. It is therefore important not to confuse normative aspects of the concept of health with the normative aspects of politically protecting and promoting population health. The fact that public health is both a scientific endeavour and a public-policy practice makes it vulnerable to such confusion.

BEING UNHEALTHY AND BEING LESS HEALTHY

As discussed before, we can talk about people being unhealthy in a comparative sense. It is important to acknowledge that we then use a different concept of health than the interpretation of health as an absence of disease; we rather mainly switch the perspective to disposition and risks. People or populations can be healthier than another person or other groups of people. They can also be healthier than they themselves were before if they are less likely to fall ill. In this respect, a person who lives in a dangerous environment or in a destitute financial situation might be less healthy than someone living in safe circumstances or someone who is wealthy.

Being less healthy is, however, not the same as suffering from ill health or being unhealthy. Being less healthy, rather, is a point on a continuum of dispositions to fall ill. If people are in good physical shape, have a strong immune system and live in an advantageous environment, then they are at the upper end of the spectrum of health. In contrasting circumstances, a person might be at the lower end, meaning she is less healthy, implying that she might be very likely to fall ill. However, it is important to appreciate that such a person is not (yet) ill because of poor health disposition. In other words, she has not fallen below the threshold of minimal health.

The point I want to make here is not merely important for conceptual clarity; it has normative significance as well. As we will see later in the book, the conceptual confusion between being unhealthy and being less healthy leads to a related confusion regarding the evaluation of the relevant conditions. Being unhealthy is bad for a person, but it is not so clear why being less healthy is also bad (in the same way). I will discuss later in a bit more detail that being less healthy might be bad in presenting a person with a disadvantage. I have also briefly mentioned that fact in an earlier section of this chapter. Disadvantage can be called a *comparative harm*, as it involves being worse off than others. Given that undeserved disadvantages are widely considered to raise claims of justice, being less healthy might still be normatively significant. Yet it is a different kind of harm involved than the absolute harm that comes with being unhealthy.

In addition, there is also a methodological issue with the very idea of being less healthy. Since it is a comparative notion, it requires a metric. A pertinent question here is in what respect a person is less healthy. It seems to make perfect sense, for instance, to compare levels of organismic functioning in different people. If someone's lung capacity, say, is better than someone else's, then this person is healthier in terms of lung capacity. However, can we ever say that a person is healthier than another as such, without any qualification? For instance, is a professional athlete who has clinical depression more healthy than a person confined to a wheelchair who is well integrated in a network of friends? This simple example instantly establishes the problem of comparing health statuses of different people. It is not just the manifold elements of individual health that make such a comparison a difficult aim to achieve but also the need for making judgements about the significance of diseases.

To be fair, research in medicine and public health partly deals with these concerns and partly ignores them for good reason. Public-health policies usually do not focus on health differences as such, but on those differences that are deemed to be of political importance. In addition, research in public health usually does not compare individuals anyway, but populations. For instance, in epidemiological studies it might be established that people with higher academic education live longer, on average, than people with a poor educational level. Here life expectancy is a proxy for general-health status within a chosen population—that is, a certain statistically generalised health-related disposition, averaged across a group of individuals. Obviously average life expectancy can be meaningfully compared between different populations. However, it should be clear that we are then talking about people being healthier than others only in a derivative sense. For normative purposes, this difference should be acknowledged.

The problem with measuring grades of health can be particularly significant when politically aiming at certain health outcomes—for instance, when an attempt is made to introduce a threshold of enough health. Any threshold, such as 'enough health', relies on a certain 'currency'—that is, an idea of what aspect of health should be targeted and up to which level it should be accessible for citizens. This is a problem that we will need to tackle more thoroughly later.

CONCLUSION

I have argued that we need to address the concept of health in its own right, not simply as an 'absence of disease'. Although I believe that publicly funded health resources should not be used—without further justification—to enhance people's health over and above the absence of disease, health is the aim of health care and public health. If we would not know what health is, we would not understand what to do when someone has a disease. Most importantly, healing a person might not always mean curing a disease.

There is a close connection between health and well-being, which is often highlighted. It might be said that health is a constitutive element of well-being. This is one reason why ill health has normative significance. Ill health is usually intrinsically bad for the person who suffers from it. Health can also be seen as an asset, as a means to other elements of well-being. Seeing health as an asset involves comparing it to other potential or real conditions, including those of other people. In this perspective, how good a person's health is depends on the health of others. Accordingly, there can be additional normative concerns that are relevant for theories of health justice. Ill health is here considered to be disadvantageous.

An important aspect of health is that it comes in grades. This potentially allows comparisons between people. In public health, we even make comparisons between different populations. Such comparisons are, however, difficult to make; they usually rely on information and data that stand as proxies for health. In addition, it is not clear, from a normative point of view, why being less healthy should have the same significance for purposes of health justice as being unhealthy.

Chapter Three

Theories of Social Justice

In the previous two chapters we have seen that good health and the absence of disease are important prerequisites and indeed elements of a flourishing and successful life. It is no surprise, then, that health has become a focal point of theories of justice. Indeed, health is not simply the object of theoretical considerations of justice. Welfare states have developed institutions to enable citizens, as much as possible, to live a healthy life. This includes medical resources provided in case of acute disease; but it also includes policies meant to prevent disease and promote health as well as to support the individual in cases where disease cannot be cured. So these days it is not simply medicine targeting citizens' health but a number of institutions dealing with seemingly unrelated issues, such as housing, employment or food safety. In other words, health is a good that is secured by many different instruments. Issues of justice in relation to human health therefore cannot be neatly separated and restricted to the allocation of medical resources. In terms of theories of justice this implies that we cannot merely set our focus to justice in medicine. To be sure, there are problems of justice that are internal to medical practice—for instance, when we consider whether to administer an expensive treatment. But a theory of health justice needs a broader remit when we discuss the provision of health-related resources on a more general level, which is sometimes called a *macro level.*

In philosophical parlance it is often said that justice is about 'what we owe to each other'. Indeed, it is important to acknowledge that claims of justice usually go along with rights. Hence, justice is not the same as charity. If people have a right to resources, then other people or institutions have the obligation to provide them, as far as possible. However, the notion of 'owing' might also generate some problematic ideas about social justice. It seems to imply that entitlements are determined by moral facts about our duties and rights, almost like an abstract debt that ought to be paid off. Such a viewpoint would ignore the historical and contextual nature of social rights. We should not forget that the provision of health care on the basis of a publicly funded system is a fairly recent development in human history and that the level of provision varies significantly in different welfare states. Health-care justice therefore seems to allow for some level of variation in reality. In addition, to owe something seems clearly different from being prepared to provide a good on grounds of humanitarian concerns or feelings of solidarity. Many acknowledged claims of justice in the real world seem to be based on the latter: They have historically developed into social obligations and hence are not merely based on charity, but neither are they owed. In brief, the slogan 'what we owe to each other' can be misleading. Nevertheless, it might help us identify a minimum of what needs to be provided as a matter of basic moral concerns.

All this raises some fairly deep issues concerning the methodology of theorising about social justice. We will return to them later in this chapter when the debate between idealism and realism in political philosophy is introduced. Before we start looking into conceptual issues surrounding the notion of social justice in the next section, it might be helpful to add another contextual element to the debate: the health status of citizens does not merely pose issues of individual and political rights and duties, to do with the kinds of harm that come with disease, but it also raises economic concerns. Partly, these are due to the economic 'burdens of disease', meaning the financial implications for welfare-state institutions dealing with individual medical harm. But economic impact is also to be seen in relation to a state's economy more generally, most importantly in terms of the workforce. Disease often leads to incapacity, and hence the health status of the citizenry is of consequence to national economies, especially given global competition. This opens up an argument for supporting the need for health-care institutions, which does not rely on concerns of justice but on economic interests. Historically it is actually not unlikely that publicly funded welfare institutions were introduced for such economic reasons, and of course other political reasons, such as supporting social cohesion and avoiding upheaval. Although the focus of this book is justice—hence basically a moral concern—the debate about the value of health cannot neatly be separated from economic interests and wider political concerns.

THE CONCEPT OF SOCIAL JUSTICE

Justice is a broad concept referring to many different concerns. For instance, we can discuss the justice of punishment or of exchanges of goods. In this study we are concerned with what is often called distributive justice. It is about the way goods and burdens are allocated between people. However, the term *distributive justice* is somewhat deficient, because issues of justice are not restricted to goods that can be distributed, in the strictest sense of the word. Health is in fact a fitting example in this respect. In political philosophy, the concept of justice usually stands for what would more correctly be called *social justice*. Briefly, the concept of social justice refers to the way society organises access to, and allocation of, specific resources, goods or benefits, and burdens.

The philosophical perspective on justice is normative. Philosophers do not primarily want to describe existing beliefs about justice or to take stock of 'what the people think'. They rather intend to establish what the right beliefs about justice are, hence what people should think about justice. This requires philosophical justification of a particular conception—a theory—of justice. As we will see in this chapter, the very task of justification of normative claims about justice might then lead some philosophers back to empirical elements of their theories after all.

The concept of justice might also apply to the whole of right action and is hence a concept of morality. Here individual acts can be deemed just or unjust. In addition, there can be an individual virtue of justice, a disposition to act in accordance with what is right. In contrast, in political philosophy it is usually institutions that are called just or unjust. Accordingly the emphasis is not on individual persons and their behaviour. Only from such a social perspective the following sentence, taken from the beginning of one of the most influential philosophical books on justice, makes sense: 'Justice is the first virtue of social institutions, as truth is of systems of thought' [1].

Moral philosophers, who usually focus on individual conduct, would rather hold that justice is a virtue (perhaps the first virtue) of persons. They might even claim that to apply the concept of virtue to institutions is a category mistake, as virtue is a character trait disposing one to act in a certain way. Institutions, in contrast, hardly have mental features. But within the perspective of political philosophy we can relax those conceptual worries and allow the concept of virtue, including the virtue of justice, to apply to social institutions. We can then see that Rawls is here actually making a normative claim, despite the apparently descriptive language ('justice *is* the first virtue of social institutions'). He does not interpret virtues as it is interpreted in moral philosophy but, rather, refers to something like an aim, purpose or goal. A proper way to interpret Rawls's influential viewpoint would therefore be to translate it thus: social institutions' foremost aim is to realise a just order. Obviously, we therefore need an account of a just order of society. In other words, we need a theory of justice. This is what political philosophers aim to achieve.

By interpreting justice as a political notion, we can also dismiss a common critique of any theory of social justice. Some scholars claimed that social justice is a 'mirage' because the concept allegedly cannot be applied to results of voluntary market exchanges. However, we can certainly discuss the political conditions leading to certain results via market transactions. For instance, if some groups of people are excluded from access to institutions of higher education, then this might be considered unjust.

We also do not need to assume that individual people have acted unjustly when discussing social justice or that individual people ought to rectify injustices. Even if no individual person can be blamed for certain conditions in society, a situation might be deemed unjust, and to meet demands of justice—providing resources—is the business of institutions. In modern societies, citizens have introduced a moral division of labour. Individual moral responsibilities to help other people, based on their entitlements, have been transferred to the state. So altogether we should not be sceptical towards the very idea of social justice.

Still, claims of justice need to be justified. A claim as such is simply a kind of demand to be provided with something, but as such it is not enough to give a claim sufficient normative force. Justified claims of justice are often also called *entitlements*, and hence they can be interpreted as rights. Health care and indeed health are often deemed rights as well. How to justify claims is therefore of utmost importance when thinking about social justice. In this study, we have already addressed some relevant issues when discussing the concepts of health and disease, as the pursuit of health and attempts to tackle disease are widely recognised to justify claims of justice. However, we have also seen that the normative basis of health justice is more complex.

Justified claims of justice are not simply those entitlements that happen to be acknowledged in a specific context. Justice is a contested notion, which implies that we can disagree about its content. The much-cited definition of the Roman jurist Ulpian, whereby justice is to render to every person their due, illustrates that what is 'due'—similarly to what we 'owe'—can be interpreted in different ways. In philosophy, we do not merely ask what is due to people in an empirical fashion—for instance, what is established as entitlements in health-care law. Rather, what is due to people here requires normative argument, meaning we should say why they should be provided with certain goods, never mind whether they actually get it. Only in this way can the concept of justice be used in a critical stance, as a tool to criticise reality.

Given that people disagree about the demands of social justice, it might be a valuable strategy to focus on formal aspects of the concept of justice. Many theorists of justice draw a close connection to impartiality and equal treatment. It seems that justice always requires us to not act arbitrarily or partially. It means to treat equal cases equally. For some, this implies a presumption in favour of equal allocation of goods, as any failure to treat people differently would need to be justified by highlighting relevant differences between cases. Consider the allocation of a cake at a birthday party: To allocate the cake justly apparently means to give everyone a slice of equal size, unless there are additional considerations justifying unequal treatment, such as special needs or desert. Equal allocation of resources hence would be the default option. This line of thinking seems to provide a strong case for a group of theories called *egalitarianism*.

However, there is a step missing here in the argument. Equal treatment is a normative requirement only in cases where it is already established that people have justified claims at all. In addition, there are normative assumptions about what constitutes relevant differences between cases that might justify unequal treatment. Consider a case where someone gives money to a beggar. Is she under an obligation to treat the next beggar she meets equally? No, she is not obliged to do so, although there are very likely no normatively relevant differences between different beggars she might meet. The reason that equal treatment is not required is that no beggar is entitled to be given money—at least, not by the person in question. Hence, the formal rule of justice to treat equal cases equally already contains substantial assumptions, most importantly that these are cases involving justified claims at all—for instance, because someone deserves something. Once it is established that there are such justified claims, equal treatment merely requires the consistent application of a rule that was established independently of concerns of equal treatment. In other words, quarrels about the content of social justice cannot be solved on grounds of formal considerations only. They have to focus on the normative basis of justified claims, such as desert, need, dignity, social status, flourishing or recognition. Once the normative basis has been established—for instance, that the presence of disease implies entitlement to the use of medical resources—then impartiality requires the application of this rule on the basis of considerations of disease only, excluding, for instance, considerations of ability to pay a contribution to medical treatment.

Impartiality might play a role on a more abstract level, though: We have established that claims of justice need to be justified. This task is what theories of justice attempt to achieve. A principle of justice, which establishes a substantial rule about how to distribute goods, needs itself to be justified impartially. Probably the best possible test for checking whether principles of justice are justified impartially is whether they can be accepted by everyone. It is no surprise, then, that universal consent is a popular aim of theories of justice. It is also the basic idea of contract theories of justice. Yet it is not obvious that a theory of justice must aim at universal consent. To be sure, it would indeed be a strong argument in favour of a particular theory of justice if it could be shown that it can secure universal approval. But aiming at consensus is not the only possible means of achieving impartial justification.

CIRCUMSTANCES OF JUSTICE

In *Enquiries Concerning the Human Understanding and Concerning the Principles of Morals*, David Hume illustrates specific circumstances that need to be present to ever apply the concept of justice; 'Thus, the rules of equity or justice depend entirely on the particular state and condition in which men are placed. . . . . Reverse, in any considerable circumstance, the condition of men: Produce extreme abundance or extreme necessity: Implant in the human breast perfect moderation and humanity, or perfect rapaciousness and malice: By rendering justice totally *useless*, you thereby totally destroy its essence, and suspend its obligation upon mankind'[2]. The second condition has to do with the subjective attitudes of people: they need to show at least some concern for others. The first condition is about the amount of resources available: they need to be moderately scarce. Altogether, the circumstances of justice describe a scenario where there is a conflict of interest between people, which requires moral rules for regulating their behaviour.

Scarcity is often implicitly identified with limitation. And it is of course true that many resources are available only in a limited amount. For instance, some natural resources like crude oil or coal are limited. But in what sense are they scarce? If we interpret scarcity as an absolute concept—that is, if we refer to limitation—then many natural and other resources are indeed scarce. Time to care for the sick is limited, as well as the number of hospital beds and medication. In health care, scarcity seems to be the norm. Accordingly, issues of justice seem to apply regularly. There is no extreme abundance or extreme necessity, both conditions Hume thought to undermine the application of rules of justice.

However, it is important to appreciate that scarcity can also be interpreted as a relational concept: resources might be scarce for someone in order to do or achieve something. In this case, it is not the limited amount of a good that makes it scarce but unrestricted demand. For instance, there could be enough medicine to treat people with specific diseases, but, given the beneficial effects of the same drug to enhance health dispositions in others as well, the required resource might be deemed scarce in relation to the claims of people. Hence, if we see scarcity in that way, then it transpires that whether a specific resource is scarce or not—and the level of scarcity as well—depend on demand as well as on supply. As we have seen in the previous chapters, in relation to the goal of health, the amount of resources we deem justified is a contested matter. In other words, the level of scarcity of health-care resources is determined by the extent of justified claims to their use. If we only focus on the supply side, then we end up with the view that all limited resources, which are in some sense instrumentally valuable and therefore of interest to people, are scarce. However, we should also focus our normative concerns on the demand side to get a full account of the real circumstances of justice.

Demand regarding a certain good, or a bundle of resources, such as health care, is influenced by at least two aspects. First, the amount of resources people consume when aiming at certain goals depends on the required level of consumption. For instance, how much time and medicine we require to fix a broken bone depends on available technology. When health-care technology makes treatment more efficient, then ill people may need fewer resources. It is no wonder, then, that economists are interested in this aspect, as it clearly seems to allow for savings. Still, technology and similar instruments' using resources more effectively and efficiently concerns only the means people require in the pursuit of certain goals, which are themselves taken for granted. The level of scarcity, in this respect, is mainly driven by factual circumstances, especially technological developments. Second, the amount of resources people consume also depends on their goals. Now, whether the ends are legitimate or justified is a normative question. It might be possible, for example, to question the legitimacy of a specific treatment because it does not show any proven medical effect.

Many theorists of justice systematically avoid raising this question of legitimate initial claims and therefore ignore an important aspect of scarcity. They only deal with the problem of how to justly distribute a certain amount of goods to people who want to have as much as possible. Claims are then justified on the basis of a maximal demand. To be sure, given the mentioned circumstances of justice, especially the limitation of goods, a demand to as many resources as possible indeed seems reasonable. After all, on such an account, all finite (and desired) goods are scarce by definition, since not all demands can be fulfilled. Hence there seems to be no basis for initially restricting normative claims, and the aim of justice seems to be to solve the interpersonal conflict of interest. However, whether the initial claim for a maximally possible share of resources should actually be acknowledged is a normative issue that needs to be raised prior to the questions dealt with by many theorists of justice.

If individual claims for the biggest possible amount of resources would not be accepted, then they might actually not be scarce—now seen from a normative perspective—because the actual supply might be able to fulfil all the justified demand. In such a perspective, whether a specific claim is justified is to be decided independently of the amount of goods available for distribution. Using the common metaphor of a cake that ought to be distributed justly, it may be possible to save a piece even where several slices of the cake are shared out. Although the cake is of a limited size, it might nevertheless not be scarce for the fulfilment of all legitimate demands. In contrast, the common viewpoint has it that because resources are limited they are scarce and therefore we need to restrict the initial maximal claims as much as possible in relation to other people's claims. The justification of individual claims in their own right is not on the agenda from this perspective. In health care, the persistent rhetoric is accordingly about rationing—restricting access to health-care resources on grounds of scarcity. However, such scarcity within the health-care system is partly of our own making.

Our discussion about the concept and the circumstances of social justice has led us to a more abstract problem: how to justify a theory of justice. This raises intricate methodological problems, which should not be avoided and will be addressed in the following sections.

GENERATING THEORIES OF JUSTICE

Like any theory, a theory of justice can be developed by different methods. It may, for instance, be reconstructed from actual social institutions or from normative beliefs identified in society. Alternatively, it can be developed on the basis of certain normative assumptions in combination with mechanisms of theory construction, such as hypothetical choices of persons. In this section, we will focus on the reconstructive and the constructive methods, as they are the most influential versions of theorising in political philosophy.

Probably the most important social institutions within single states to be linked to criteria of social justice are the legal constitution and elements of the welfare state. A theory of justice built by the method of reconstruction accordingly studies these political institutions and attempts to distil a particular account of a normative social order. This might be done in a mainly descriptive manner—for instance, by analysing real welfare states. An influential philosophical variant of the method of reconstructing a theory of justice can be found in Michael Walzer's *Spheres of Justice*[3], where he develops a theory by way of interpreting a real society, the United States, especially in terms of the way citizens themselves see the significance of particular goods and how they want to organise access to these goods. Walzer is interested in 'what the people think', to use the catchy phrase of one of his followers, David Miller[4]. Walzer focuses on specific social goods—for instance, welfare, leisure, work and so on—and reconstructs a multispherical theory of justice by way of interpreting the goods and their nature in combination with people's beliefs about these goods. A variant of such a method can be found in Axel Honneth's recent work on social freedom, *Freedom's Right*[5]. He is more historically minded than Walzer and refers to actual social struggles over the right way to organise institutions—most importantly, the market, the family and the law.

The reconstructive method usually allows for a plurality of viewpoints on justice. Surely theorists using this method have additional criteria to favour a particular theory—for instance, because it fits better with normative beliefs of actual people. Some possible theories might even be ruled out on such an account because they do not fulfil some minimal normative criteria or because they are infeasible. But according to the reconstructive method, there is not only one right theory of justice but several. This is an important difference from the constructive method, which we will deal with shortly.

From the perspective of many political philosophers, the reconstructive method fails to account for the specific normativity of the concept of justice. Walzer's interpretative account appears to merely lead to a summary of actual normative beliefs. In other word, the method seems to lead to conservatism or conventionalism. Yet a theory of justice cannot simply be justified by claiming that it is the one people believe to be right. We will see later in this section—when focussing more directly on issues of justification—that the success of such an objection depends, however, on a fairly rigid distinction between issues of normative justification and empirical description. In addition, one might wonder on what basis justification of an account of justice might be grounded if not on normative beliefs of real people and facts about the world.

An important alternative to a reconstructive method in political philosophy is the constructive method. Here a theory of justice is generated by certain basic assumptions and mechanisms of theory generation. Basic assumptions can be both descriptive and normative. For instance, every (convincing) theory of justice grounds on an assumption of the moral equality of all human beings. There might be empirical assumptions that are themselves contested—for example, about the role of incentives in the motivational structure of persons or about the scarcity of certain goods.

John Rawls, who has already been mentioned as one of the most influential philosophers of social justice, used a constructive method. In order to generate principles of justice he assumed a fair-choice situation in which parties were supposed to choose principles for themselves. Hence this method does not simply describe or interpret what citizens actually prefer or institutionalise in their societies but, rather, models a hypothetical choice situation. Obviously this initial situation needs to be adequate for the task of generating principles of justice. It is thus unlikely that the choice of the involved parties could be unrestricted. In Rawls's theory, the choice situation, which he dubs the *original position*, restricts the parties' knowledge about their actual social status, their gender, their economic income and so on. This is because Rawls plausibly assumes that on the basis of selfish motivations we will not be able to generate just principles. He claims that from the description of the just-choice situation in combination with theoretical assumptions about the parties' motives specific principles will follow. The content of these principles is not relevant here, as we are interested in methodological issues. Rawls's specific theory of justice follows from his model of a fair-choice situation. Accordingly, he describes his conception as 'justice as fairness'.

Ronald Dworkin, another well-known political philosopher, offers a similar constructive account[6]. He assumes a situation of no prior rights attached to resources, illustrated by shipwrecked people landing on an island. Since individuals have different preferences and conceptions of their own good, allocation of resources should be based on individual choices. This is modelled by setting an initially fair situation in which everyone gets an equal share of convertible possessions, representing a currency of some kind; in Dworkin's model these are clamshells from the beach. Currency is then traded on a market into preferred goods and services. Prices for these goods are established via auction, and certain insurances are established for disadvantages due to bad luck not resulting from people's own choices—for instance, disabilities. Eventually this hypothetical society will allocate resources to individuals until nobody envies any other person's bundle of resources. A just allocation is the result, according to Dworkin. Again, as in Rawls's theory, he uses a method we can call *constructive* because it includes certain assumptions about an initially fair situation and mechanisms of letting people determine for themselves what they deem substantially just.

Utilitarianism can also be seen as following a constructive method as it builds on an axiom, the principle of utility, and adds certain mechanisms of calculation, including standards of assessment and aggregation. This method is supposed to determine just institutions. An important difference from Rawls's and Dworkin's model is that utilitarianism does not require individuals themselves to choose certain principles or outcomes as just but, rather, involves individual preferences merely as data in an objective calculation that might, for instance, be performed by an impartial spectator. The latter individual is of course a counterfactual, though possible, device of theory construction. Utilitarianism is a philosophical theory well established in ethics, but it is also applied to issues of social justice. Many accounts in economic theory have been heavily influenced by utilitarianism, especially in social-choice theory.

To be sure, there are more methods than those mentioned so far. For example, similarly to in theories in the natural sciences, political philosophers might assume a normative reality or a theory of essences or ideas, as in Plato's *Republic*. According to such a method, a theory of justice mirrors the real world of justice, albeit in an imperfect way. We may call this subject-external account a method of discovery. It has become unfashionable in political philosophy for obvious reasons, most importantly because we do not have direct epistemic access to such a normative world, even if we would believe in its existence. The method of discovery, hence, does not find many supporters in philosophy these days. To be sure, it should be acknowledged that the main problems for such an approach are chiefly due to its assumed basis of justification. It is certainly possible to generate a theory of justice including elements that are not at all related to subjective beliefs. Still, it is hard to see how its prescriptions might be justified to people if these do not seem reasonable in their opposing views on justice. Nevertheless, such a method of developing a theory of justice was influential for quite some time, in the Western world beginning with Plato, according to our recorded knowledge. There are also echoes of such thinking in natural-law theory, which still has defenders today. But for most theorists, the idea of justice is an invention of human beings. It seems difficult to generate and justify a normative theory without any reference to peoples' beliefs.

Both the reconstructive and the constructive methods see justice in close connection to choices of people. The main difference consists in how they model the involved parties and institutions. Whereas the reconstructive method relies to a significant degree on reality—although these theories necessarily involve a certain amount of abstraction and generalisations—constructive models build in idealisations and normative assumptions right from the start. This brings us to the important issue of justification.

JUSTIFYING THEORIES OF JUSTICE

A possible rationale for considering a theory of justice to be justified would be directly analogous to a theory in empirical sciences. We can test the latter type of theories against reality, and, although we might never end up in a justification 'once and for all', we still have valid reasons for preferring one theory over another on the basis of how well it fits reality. But, as mentioned before, in the normative domain there does not seem to be such reality, or at least we do not have epistemic access to any normative reality even if we might assume that it exists. Given this situation, the best basis for justification seems to be consensus. Indeed, the best justification of a normative theory consists in the convergence of the normative beliefs of all people. If everybody would agree with a particular theory of justice in a free and informed choice, theorists would seem to have all they could reasonably hope for when aiming at justification of normative claims.

Perhaps the intuitive pull of such a method of justification has led to the privileged position of contract theory in political philosophy. However, the price of such a method is its necessary abstraction from reality. After all, in reality, people—even if sufficiently reasonable and informed—do not agree on particular principles of justice, or on any version of the welfare state, for that matter, as being just. The way to deal with this factual lack of consensus in most normative theories of justice is to introduce an idealised account of justification. This account might be based, again, on an ideal situation of collective choice or common deliberation. Alternatively, it might rely on the convergence of individual normative beliefs of people who have reached an ideal situation of deliberation about issues of justice. The latter idea has been called—by John Rawls—*reflective equilibrium*, and it has received considerable support in normative philosophical theory as a method of justification. We will look at this model more closely.

Reflective equilibrium can be called a subject-internal state that is accomplished by a method of reflection guided by the criterion of coherence. The elements brought into coherence in reflective equilibrium are, however, not merely subjective, or perhaps even purely intuitive, beliefs. The relevant judgements are supposed to be considered judgements; they are critically scrutinised in the light of moral principles and background theories. Considered judgements are therefore judgements made in specific circumstances, without distorting influences on deliberative abilities and untainted by egoistic interests. 'Considered judgements', writes Rawls, 'are simply those rendered under conditions favourable to the exercise of the sense of justice, and therefore in circumstances where the more common excuses and explanations for making a mistake do not obtain'[7].

But why should the fact that our judgements have the quality of being considered render them more trustworthy or normatively authoritative? Obviously people can hold considered judgements that are clearly morally outrageous. Richard Brandt objects to Rawls, writing that 'the fact that a person has a firm normative conviction gives that belief a status no better than fiction'. He adds that Rawls's method only leads to a 'reshuffling of moral prejudices'[8]. Accordingly, he demands that the constraints of normative belief formation, set by social and cultural influences, be broken and that alternative viewpoints be engaged at least hypothetically. Only then, he says, will people reach trustworthy normative judgements. However, the charge of conventionalism against Rawls, implicit in Brandt's objection, is not valid. For Rawls, considered moral judgements are not the final authority of justification. The reflective method does not merely aim at an internally coherent viewpoint. Other considerations, independent of an individual person's point of view, are also to be included—namely, theoretical insights. Every single considered judgement can come under scrutiny in reflective equilibrium and has to withstand the test. Hence, 'there are no judgements on any level of generality that are in principle immune to revision'[9].

To make the inclusion of background theories within the method of justification more explicit, Rawls later distinguished between narrow and wide reflective equilibrium. Narrow reflective equilibrium achieves internal order and coherence between a person's beliefs. Some individual judgements may conflict with a person's principled beliefs, but the conflicts merely set the task to sort out conflicts within ourselves. In wide reflective equilibrium, which is still an equilibrium of beliefs of individual persons, there are a couple of further considerations added to the search for a balance: these might be philosophical considerations—for example, about human agency, the nature of persons and the role of morality but also scientific facts and theories, such as findings concerning the mechanisms of economic markets.

So altogether we get, in the succinct summary offered by Norman Daniels, an account of wide reflective equilibrium: 'The method of wide reflective equilibrium is an attempt to produce coherence in an ordered triple of sets of beliefs held by a particular person, namely, (a) a set of considered moral judgments, (b) a set of moral principles, and (c) a set of relevant background theories'[10].

So far this is an account of individual epistemic justification. It justifies an individual person to hold certain beliefs due to being in a state of wide reflective equilibrium. Now, it is still possible that people hold different sets of such coherent beliefs. In relation to Rawlsian-theory elements, for example, some persons might hold the original position to be a good description of the constraints when choosing principles of justice, while others might coherently support another account of the initial-choice situation. It is not likely that there will be only one version of individual wide reflective equilibrium people end up settling on after due reflection. Any particular normative claim supposed to be justified by the method of reflective equilibrium requires the convergence of individual reflective equilibria. If such convergence is given, Rawls speaks of a general reflective equilibrium. This is the real aim of justification in normative theory. Here we do not simply ask whether persons are epistemically justified to hold certain beliefs. Rather, in justifying a normative theory we aim at a convergence of the individual beliefs. If all individual reflective equilibria agree on one particular theory of justice, it can be deemed justified. The object of justification is a theory, not beliefs.

But one might wonder whether the convergence of individual reflective equilibria is at all likely. In other words, is a general reflective equilibrium possible? There are two different routes in Rawls's writings to achieving a general reflective equilibrium. The first route employs specific idealisations, especially an assumption regarding a well-ordered society. This route settles the issue by stipulation. The second route is more realistic but apparently ends in wishful thinking. To understand some of the tensions between ideal normative political philosophy and more realistically minded approaches, it is instructive to look more closely at the two routes available to Rawls.

The idealist argument for general reflective equilibrium consists in the claim that in a well-ordered society all parties agree on the same conception of justice. 'Recall that a well-ordered society is a society effectively regulated by a public conception of justice. Think of each citizen in such a society as having achieved wide (versus narrow) reflective equilibrium. But since citizens recognise that they affirm the same public conception of political justice, reflective equilibrium is also general: the same conception is affirmed in everyone's considered judgements'[11]. This, of course, simply begs the question. Rawls's conception of justice is allegedly justified in general reflective equilibrium, but general reflective equilibrium can only be secured by reference to the idea of a well-ordered society, which is nothing more than a theoretical stipulation. Therefore, this argument for general reflective equilibrium is a nonstarter.

By taking the other route, Rawls claims that he merely describes a possible convergence in the reflective equilibria of persons. He adopts the role of an 'observing moral theorist'[12] and does not prescribe particular judgements; neither does he refer to them as the only correct ones. Rather, Rawls claims that people actually converge in their beliefs when they are in wide reflective equilibrium. His theory of justice, according to this reading, is justified because of the fact that people do really accept it in an ideal deliberative condition. In this reading, his method of reflective equilibrium is a test of the 'psychological fit' between normative theoretical claims and normative beliefs of people. But to claim that this is indeed the case is, again, just an assertion that seems to be based on wishful thinking. To be sure, the convergence might be established, but only if we could empirically check its truth value. As long as people have not all reached wide reflective equilibrium, it is merely an unfounded claim that his theory of justice would be preferred to other conceptions.

Altogether, Rawls's method of reflective equilibrium is an example of how empirical findings might have an impact on developing a convincing normative political theory—in his case, a theory of justice. Background theories are at least partly empirical in that they include data, such as psychological findings about the structure of human motivation. More importantly, his account, at least in one possible interpretation, also includes reference to facts about normative beliefs of people. This seems, after all, an important ingredient in any model of justification in political philosophy.

In summary, the way we generate and justify theories of social justice has important repercussions on how we think about entitlements in real life. Clashes of opinions in what is just are often based on such foundational methodological issues. It is, hence, important to understand the basic differences between philosophical theories of justice, especially as regards the distinction between constructive and reconstructive approaches. It is also vital to understand different interpretations of the reflective procedure leading to a justified theory of justice, which can form the basis of justified claims for gaining guaranteed access to resources. I have suggested that there will likely be persistent and reasonable differences in people's interpretations of what is just. It is unlikely that there will be one and only one theory of social justice that will stand the philosophical test. After all, social justice is a notion closely related to real political struggles and institutions.

EGALITARIANISM

In *Inequality Reexamined*, Amartya Sen asserts that 'every normative theory of social arrangement that has at all stood the test of time seems to demand equality of something'[13]. If this were correct, then egalitarianism would appear to be in a privileged position and we would only need ask what kind of equality we should opt for. However, 'Equality of what?' is not the only reasonable question that arises when discussing issues of social justice. As we will see shortly, 'Why equality?' is another important problem.

Egalitarianism is a label that can be used for many different theories. Partly, this versatility might be responsible for Sen's claim regarding the privileged position of egalitarianism. However, we should not gloss over relevant differences between theories of justice. It is important, then, to distinguish different ideas of equality that are affiliated with relevant theories.

Egalitarianism can be understood as referring to those theories that aim at equal moral statuses among citizens or all human beings. To show equal respect and concern indeed has been acknowledged widely as a basic moral demand that applies to people and institutions. In this respect it might indeed be correct to assume that every normative theory of social arrangement is egalitarian. But surely theorists disagree about what equality of respect and concern means in terms of the allocation of goods within societies—that is, in terms of social justice.

Within the context of social-justice theories, egalitarianism should be understood as referring to those accounts that aim at distributional equality of some kind. They demand equality of something—for instance, of specific resources or of less tangible goods, such as welfare, opportunities or capabilities. Differences within the egalitarian camp therefore concern the so-called currencies of justice; but all these theories aim at securing equal amounts of the relevant currency for each citizen—or for each human being if they are global egalitarians.

Egalitarianism has strong intuitive appeal because being worse off than others in a relevant respect without one's own fault clearly seems to be unjust. Institutions should therefore aim at supporting those people in worse positions than others and work to get them back to level terms. Poor health is an obvious example in this respect, as it seems unjust if people with a disease are not offered or cannot afford treatment. Note, however, that egalitarianism regarding health does not demand giving equal amounts of publicly funded health-care resources to every citizen. Rather, the aim is equality of health status, and that means giving health-care resources to those people who are ill, relative to their level of illness. Egalitarianism accordingly sets a goal to strive at—equality in relation to a specific currency. Since some people are in an advantaged position relative to others, equalising the positions of all regularly requires allocating goods unequally in order to achieve equality. Egalitarianism has therefore occasionally been described as focusing on end states—as opposed to historical theories, which focus on the causation of allocations of goods within societies, mainly by free individual exchange of goods.

Although it is correct to state that equality of some kind is the goal of egalitarianism, the labelling as end-state theories can cause confusion, as historical elements regarding the causation of inequality do also play a role in egalitarian thinking. We have just seen that egalitarians usually hold that undeserved inequalities constitute injustices. Hence, within such a theory it must be determined whether an inequality is based on free decisions people have made or they are to be blamed for being in a disadvantageous position. In other words, egalitarians often draw a distinction between inequalities resulting from brute (bad) luck that accordingly raise issues of justice and inequalities caused by free decisions—sometimes referred to as *option luck*. The latter situations do not raise concerns of justice, as people are to be held responsible for their own free decisions. At least, this is the basic idea of so-called luck egalitarianism. Obviously, the distinction between option luck and brute luck raises pertinent philosophical concerns. We will discuss these in the next chapter in relation to the specific problem of individual responsibility for health status. It seems difficult to determine the level of individual contribution, in contrast to circumstantial elements, in all choices. It also seems cruel to leave people in dire straits, even if it is clearly their fault that they ended up in this situation. Modern welfare states moved away from notions such as 'deserving poor' for good reason. So perhaps equality of some kind should not be the only value pursued by a theory of social justice.

To be sure, egalitarianism need not include an element of responsibility or desert. It can aim at straight equality in terms of some relevant currency. Here equality is seen as a value in its own right that should not be compromised. So-called *telic egalitarianism* accordingly holds that it is intrinsically bad if people are unequal in terms of a relevant currency. Such a monistic view, however, which only aims at equality of some kind without taking other elements into consideration, seems doomed to failure. Most importantly, it seems to require the worsening of the position of the advantaged group even where this does not lead to an improvement of the position of the disadvantaged group. Consider a current allocation of housing where some people have three bedrooms and some two bedrooms. They cannot be made equal by reallocating fractions of bedrooms. Still, equality of bedrooms could be achieved by blocking access to one bedroom for the advantaged group. But this seems unreasonable. This example, although hypothetical, provides the gist of the so-called *levelling-down objection* to some versions of egalitarianism. The levelling-down objection mainly shows that equality alone will probably not constitute a convincing theory of social justice. Egalitarianism needs to be a pluralistic theory, adding elements of efficiency or utility, and perhaps also elements of responsibility and minimal welfare, to the concern of equality.

In his theory of justice John Rawls started his argument from an egalitarian plateau, which meant that his initial idea was that everyone should have equal amounts of so-called social primary goods—such as rights, liberties and income. For some of these goods, especially income, Rawls assumed more would be available if inequalities were allowed to exist. The basic idea behind this was that earning more is an incentive for people to be more productive. Accordingly, some inequalities could be justified on grounds of economic thinking. Rawls added in one of his principles of justice, the so-called *difference principle*, that inequalities would need to be beneficial to the least-advantaged group in society. Again, the idea was that in virtue of the economic growth almost all would benefit and that inequalities in income could be justified if the specific focus on the worst off would be kept. Rawls's difference principle has stirred up a lot of debate. For our purpose it suffices to introduce his idea as a version of so-called prioritarianism, which has been established as a group of theories of social justice in its own right.

Prioritarianism, as it has just been defined, can be argued to be a version of egalitarianism, which combines egalitarian concerns with an additional element of justice: economic efficiency. Seen from this angle, prioritarianism is not really in conflict with egalitarianism. Rather, it addresses a specific gap in straightforward egalitarian thinking—namely, situations that might raise the level of welfare for many but also involve inequalities. Here it seems that the reasonable option would be to combine egalitarian with additional concerns. If the specific mix introduces a normative priority for the worse-off, or indeed the worst off, then this is a version of prioritarianism.

To be sure, it should be said that most prioritarians see themselves in opposition to egalitarianism. This mainly has to do with the fact that their main concern is about absolute positions of people within a distributive scheme, not their relative position in comparison to others. As we will see, this particular concern brings them closer to sufficientarianism. Altogether, such detail again confirms that knowledge of labels for theories alone does not suffice to comprehend the theoretical landscape.

So far egalitarianism has been introduced as a theory aiming at equality of amounts of specific goods, whether tangible goods, such as specific resources, or more abstract goods, such as welfare. There are also versions of egalitarianism that do not focus directly on goods but on relationships between people. This idea is closely connected to the notion of moral equality. People can be considered equal when they have the same moral and social statuses. Now, this can imply many different aspects and opens up new avenues for thinking about justice. Being considered to be of lower worth by one's fellow citizens, being discriminated against or being excluded from socially recognised spheres of production can all be seen as implied unjust inequalities not, or not directly, based on distributional issues. Consider the example of people with disabilities: They might have access to resources that secure equal opportunities for them in many areas of life, but they might nevertheless be unequal insofar as they are considered deficient in bodily appearance. Such potential social injustices can be identified by considerations about the relationship between citizens. Hence this perspective is considered to lay the foundation for an alternative form of egalitarianism focussing on relational equality.

There is an ongoing dispute in political philosophy regarding whether different versions of egalitarianism—specifically luck egalitarianism and relational egalitarianism—are really in opposition. It is true, as has been stated, that the one focuses more on the situation of individuals—on their assets and access to goods—whereas the other focuses on the interpersonal, relational aspects. But these aspects could perhaps be combined in a pluralistic version of egalitarianism.

NONEGALITARIANISM

Not everyone is convinced that social justice means people should have equal amounts of goods. 'The fundamental error of egalitarianism lies in supposing that it is morally important whether one person has less than another regardless of how much either of them has'[14]. Harry Frankfurt has been a vocal critic of egalitarianism. He has also developed an alternative approach, called *sufficientarianism*—basically, a theory of justice aiming at everyone's having enough of some relevant goods. In this section we will focus on the destructive element, which emerges from the question, 'Why equality?'

It has already been stated that equality of moral status is not at issue here. Nonegalitarianism is concerned with distributional and relational aspects. It claims that social justice does not require equality in these respects. To be sure, there might be situations in which justice results when everyone has been allocated an equal amount of goods—for instance, when they have the same level of need. But equal distribution in this case is not the direct aim of social justice; it is a contingent consequence of people getting what they need. To better understand the difference between egalitarianism and nonegalitarianism, it is advisable to briefly discuss the notion of equality.

Equality is a tripartite relation. There are two things to compare—as regards justice, this is usually individual people or groups—and a standard of comparison. For instance, person A and person B might be equal in terms of their income. So the standard of comparison would be the currency of a version of egalitarianism, such as opportunities, welfare, capabilities and the like. Now, the standard of comparison might be scalar—that is, allow for different grades. Income is an obvious example, but also positive health, as explained in the previous chapter. Whether people are equal in terms of gradable standards depends on their comparative standing. Alternatively, the standard of comparison might be nonscalar, or absolute. For instance, we might compare people's respective right to vote. It is either the case or not; the interpersonal comparison between people does not pertain to their equality in the relevant respect. We might want to call this kind of equality *noncomparative*.

It is important to realise that every scalar measure—or every currency of social justice—can be transferred into a noncomparative standard, simply by setting a threshold that everyone is supposed to reach. For instance, one could define a minimal income or a minimal level of health that ought to be secured by social institutions for every citizen as a matter of justice. Defining such a threshold implies leaving the egalitarian point of view, as the comparative position between people is deemed normatively insignificant, whereas egalitarianism by definition is concerned with relative positions. In Frankfurt's terms, quoted at the beginning of this section, a nonegalitarian account of justice maintains that it is not morally important whether or not one person has less than another but, rather, how much either of them has. This is the starting point for a group of theories of social justice grouped under the label *sufficientarianism*.

If we categorise theories of justice that opt for a nonscalar currency of justice as nonegalitarian—as I have suggested—then relational egalitarianism is not straightforwardly a version of egalitarianism. After all, despite the fact that it focusses on relationships between people, it usually sets thresholds of inclusion, such as feeling like a valued member of society or living a dignified life. Nevertheless, relational equality might also contain comparative standards—for instance, political power. To make things even more complicated, noncomparative standards might themselves be driven by comparative considerations. What it means to lead a dignified life might be partly determined by the level of well-being that other people have achieved. Still, the standard—once set—is the aim to be met by everyone as a matter of justice. Whether people do indeed meet the target of a dignified life is then independent of their comparative standing relative to others.

The debate about egalitarianism and nonegalitarianism has shown that we need to be careful how we use labels. It is important, of course, to understand differences between types of theories, but usually real philosophical theories do not neatly fall into either camp. A convincing egalitarian theory of justice is not only concerned with persons having less than others but also with how much they all have. A good example of these mixed concerns is the notion of poverty, which can be seen in absolute terms and as a comparative, or relative, standard. Many theories of justice would see both absolute and relative poverty as an issue of injustice, up to a point. For nonegalitarian theories, relative poverty is not a normative concern unless it undermines the achievement of other nonscalar standards of justice—say, minimal education. Hence comparative aspects might be indirectly significant from a nonegalitarian perspective.

Another influential theory of justice that could be deemed nonegalitarian is argued by Michael Walzer, who aims at *complex equality*, which basically means that justice prevails when citizens hold different positions in separate spheres of justice. Equality is here again understood as a basic moral goal, not a direct distributional demand; hence, Walzer's theory is not a version of egalitarianism. In fact, he allows for numerous distributional and relational principles of justice, determined by interpretations of the goods under consideration—for example, work, leisure or education. As explained above, this is a reconstructive approach, but here it is more important to add that it is a pluralist theory of justice. As long as spheres are being kept separate and do not dominate others by invading the criteria of just allocation, a society can be deemed just.

Finally, another prominent nonegalitarian group of theories is grouped under the label *libertarianism*. Given the name, it is probably not surprising that the main focus of justice for libertarians is liberty—or individual freedom, to use a less politically connotated word. Libertarianism is sometimes considered antiegalitarian, especially since many people believe that freedom and equality are conflicting values. This, however, is debatable. It is true, of course, that in order to maintain welfare institutions, such as subsidised schools or indeed a universal system of health care, material resources are needed, which are usually generated by taxes. The duty to pay taxes can of course be seen as a coercive instrument of the state. Robert Nozick, leading proponent of libertarianism, called taxation 'on a par with forced labour'[15]. However, welfare institutions are normally enabling institutions; they aim to secure the constant maintenance of individual freedom for all citizens by addressing common risks of human life that undermine the individual ability to lead a free life, such as ignorance, illness, unemployment and so on. Insofar as the welfare state maintains individual freedom for all, it is harder to see why taxation is on a par with forced labour. It is rather on a par with compulsory insurance, which might still be problematic, of course. But at least a system of insurance makes clear that the beneficiaries of taxation are all citizens together, which can hardly be compared with the practice of forced labour. Acknowledging this, it is also less clear why freedom should be seen in conflict to the value of equality, at least when interpreting equality as basic moral equality. Enabling citizens by securing individual freedom in view of common threats basically means aiming at achieving equal respect.

Libertarianism might now look like an antisocial theory after all—perhaps not even worthy of being called a theory of social justice—as it seems to be concerned merely with nonnegotiable individual claims against one another, obviously favourable to citizens who can afford to maintain their freedom without relying on others. But there are versions of libertarianism that allow for freedom as a currency of justice and are not merely stumbling blocks for the application of any principle of justice. These versions are commonly called *left libertarianism*, alluding to widespread stereotypes about political camps. Many libertarians acknowledge that in order to be really free one needs resources and to stand in certain relation to others, most importantly a relation of nondomination. Accordingly, social justice from this perspective demands securing real freedom for all. Since there does not seem to be one specific resource that can secure individual freedom in deeply pluralistic societies, it seems adequate to aim at a convertible good—most importantly, money—as a proxy for the level of individual freedom. At this point, some left-libertarian theories of social justice might seem very similar to egalitarian accounts. However, as mentioned before, equal distribution within libertarianism is a contingent outcome of assumptions about what is required to secure real freedom for all. Equal distribution is not a direct aim of this account.

SUFFICIENTARIANISM

So far we have focused on egalitarianism and its critics. A natural development from Frankfurt's objection that equality does not matter morally is his idea that everyone should have enough. Accordingly, a theory of justice developed from this perspective would aim at sufficient levels of the relevant currencies of justice. 'What is important from the point of view of morality is not that everyone should have the same, but that each should have enough. If everyone had enough, it would be of no moral consequence whether one had more than others'[16]. As we have already seen, it is not straightforward whether Frankfurt's second claim would be right even if we granted his first. Whether one has more than others might well be of indirect moral consequence. For instance, if someone is better educated than others and in virtue of that advantage has a higher chance of staying healthy, we might see this as evidence of injustice and accordingly reconsider standards of sufficiency. In our example, this might mean raising the standard of sufficient 'health literacy' that ought to be secured for every citizen, enabling them to make healthy choices or making information about nutritional content of food more available and easier to grasp. Such indirect concerns would still allow us to stay within the sufficientarian perspective.

As we have just seen, sufficientarianism aims at securing enough goods of the relevant currency for everyone. In other words, sufficientarianism necessarily involves an account of what is enough. This might be very difficult to articulate in substantive terms. For instance, how much education should everyone be able to achieve? In addition, the focus on 'enough' generates the important question, 'Enough of what, exactly?' We will return to the latter question in the final chapter, when a sufficientarian account of health justice is presented in more detail. The other problem, determining what 'enough' means, has already been tackled in previous chapters, at least up to a point, in the context of health care. Health justice means securing, as far as possible, minimal health—that is, the absence of illness.

There is another important problem for sufficientarianism that admittedly applies to any theory of justice. It needs to be specified to whom 'everyone' refers. Most welfare states aim to enable citizens of the state to lead their own lives independently. Citizens, again, can all be residents who live in a particular country or all people who hold a relevant passport. However, if the aim of social justice is to secure enough for everyone, such restrictions of the group of beneficiaries do not seem straightforward. For instance, if minimal health is required in order to live a decent life, why should it matter whether a person holds a particular passport or lives in a specific country? In other words, should principles of social justice instead apply globally? We will return to this question in a later chapter and ignore it for the purposes of this chapter.

Sufficientarianism follows a different rationale than egalitarianism, since it focusses on noncomparative standards, whereas egalitarianism is necessarily concerned with comparative aspects. Sufficientarianism determines what is due to people on the basis of a set standard, not on the basis of what other people have. Still, as we have seen earlier, it may allow for egalitarian demands in addition to sufficientarian ones; hence sufficientarianism is not necessarily in direct competition with egalitarianism. Only if we follow both of Frankfurt's conjectures cited above—that is, if we say that it only matters that people have enough and not at all whether one has more than the other—would the theories be incompatible.

The difference between a comparative and noncomparative perspective is not often acknowledged in theories of social justice. The distinction between two respective forms of justice goes back to Joel Feinberg, who writes, 'In all cases, of course, justice consists in giving a person his due, but in some cases one's due is determined independently of that of other people, while in other cases, a person's due is determinable *only* by reference to his relations to other persons. I shall refer to contexts, criteria, and principles of the former kind as *noncomparative*, and those of the latter sort as *comparative*'[17].

Following Feinberg's distinction, we can describe the general idea of justice by the following principle: *For all X that fulfil criterion Y, Z is due.* This can be specified in various ways. For instance, a theory of health justice might claim that all citizens with a family member who developed breast cancer should have access to free additional early detection programs. This would be a noncomparative principle of justice. Whether the relevant criterion is fulfilled by a person depends on her circumstances only. Alternatively, we might hold that only 5 percent of the population with the highest risk of getting breast cancer should get this additional access. Whether one gets additional screening for free in this second scenario depends on the health risk of other people. It is therefore a comparative principle of justice.

In addition to sufficientarian concerns of justice, there might be considerations demanding comparative principles, especially in competitive scenarios. Levelling the playing field regularly involves comparative aspects, such as the level of skills of competitors or their relative advantage. Similarly, there might be concerns of comparative justice when considering the level of health of citizens. For instance, we might hold that it is unjust if rich people live longer than others because they have access to better living conditions and more advanced health care. Accordingly, there might be egalitarian concerns in addition to sufficientarian ones. This might be especially fitting because health seems to have competitive aspects, which are summarised in its instrumental value, as explained in the previous chapters.

To be sure, some of the egalitarian concerns may be adequately described either by a sufficientarian perspective or dealt with by other means than egalitarian reallocation of relevant goods. Sufficientarianism may require an equal distribution of goods because it might happen that everyone should have access to the same amount of a certain good. Equal distribution, in these cases, is a contingent consequence of a noncomparative principle, not its direct aim. In addition, some egalitarian concerns might be dealt with by putting up fences between different spheres of justice, as explained in Walzer's theory. If access to health care or to healthy environments were not based at all on ability to pay or on level of education, current concerns about rich people tending to live longer or similar inequalities could probably be met. Altogether, sufficientarianism looks like a strong contender.

Nevertheless, there are several objections to sufficientarianism. For instance, some authors claim that the threshold of sufficiency, usually described as aimed at securing a decent life, implies that a life below such a standard is not worth living. But this does not follow. Whether a life is worth living to the person in question is necessarily based on her subjective evaluation. The evaluation only applies to one particular person. Sufficientarianism, in contrast, determines a threshold that concerns the conditions for a decent life; in that respect it is not based merely on individual evaluations. Where a person is located on a scale of well-being says nothing about the worth of living that life. Obviously a life could be considered not worth living even for a person living way above the threshold. All sufficientarianism claims is that a life below the threshold means enduring bad or indecent living conditions.

Another objection that many authors are concerned with is that the threshold set by sufficientarianism would need to be either ambiguous or arbitrary. Arbitrariness is of course the very contradiction of justice. But surely there is an important difference between indeterminacy and arbitrariness; these should not be confused. If the threshold should prove to be indeterminate or ambiguous, this is not undermining its rational status within a theory of justice. What is left indeterminate in a theory of justice can be determined by real decisions within society. This renders the threshold nonarbitrary as well.

Again, some complain that sufficientarianism does not deal with unjust conditions above the threshold and implies dubious allocations below the threshold, because resources might be 'wasted' in the attempt to bring people up to the threshold. This objection is based on confusion, although it has to be said that some supporters of sufficientarianism are also guilty of this misguided thinking. The objection relies on an inadequate description of the very purpose of sufficientarianism—namely, allegedly making comparative evaluations between different possible allocations of goods. Sufficientarianism allegedly assumes that it matters more that people have enough than that other concerns are addressed, or that priority should be given to the badly off. This is correct, in a sense, but nevertheless inadequate; it is correct insofar as sufficientarianism indeed claims that it is important that people have enough but does not imply that it matters more than other normative concerns or that indeed other aspects of justice do not matter at all. There can be a change in the sorts of reasons when we argue about matters of justice, and sufficientarianism is based on particular reasons. Sufficientarian reasons address what a just distribution of goods looks like, not how just distribution compares to other possible distributions. The latter concern exceeds the claims of sufficientarianism—for, instance regarding the aggregation of different units of goods.

In sum, in this section I have introduced sufficientarianism as a noncomparative theory of justice. It does not rule out additional comparative facets of justice; it is not simply concerned with these as a matter of philosophical theory. Such a sufficientarian approach aims at setting a threshold of social justice, of what is enough. Surely it is possible that citizens might want to secure for everyone a level of provision above what is merely enough on a noncomparative basis—for instance, because they want to live in an equitable society. Sufficientarianism does not undermine this desire; it merely states that this is not its concern and that it remains to be seen whether such an additional demand of distributional equality can be justified as a matter of justice or whether it is more of a matter of political preference.

Whether sufficientarianism can only secure levels of minimal provision depends on the level set by the threshold of 'enough'. As regards the context of health care and the social determinants of health, it seems that even the threshold of securing minimal health for everyone can be a demanding doctrine. In a later chapter we will aim to flesh out the idea of enough health for all in a bit more detail.

CONCLUSION

Health justice needs to be discussed in the context of theories of social justice. In this chapter, we have introduced numerous types of theories. An important distinction, which will have relevance in later chapters as well, can be drawn between comparative and noncomparative justice. Egalitarianism is a theory of comparative justice; sufficientarianism is a theory of noncomparative justice.

Theories of social justice usually put forward normative principles as to which goods should be made available to people in what way. Principles state the substantive content of a theory. Merely formal principles, such as the duty to treat people impartially, cannot alone decide issues of social justice. Similarly, putative facts regarding the circumstances of justice are normatively loaded and hence cannot be used to predetermine what theories are most plausible. The fact that there are indeed numerous different theories of social justice to be found in political philosophy led us to more abstract considerations regarding the methodology of such theories. Here we have distinguished between a reconstructive and a constructive method. Importantly, these differ in terms of how much they include political realities.

A widespread model to justify theories of justice is reflective equilibrium. This requires that we balance considered normative judgements with principles and theoretical assumptions into a coherent set of beliefs. Since normative problems, such as devising and justifying a theory of justice, do not allow for straightforward factual tests to determine the best available theory, reflective equilibrium seems to be our best available model of scrutiny. But, again, it is not exactly clear what this amounts to. I have argued that there will always be persistent and reasonable differences about social justice; these cannot be solved by philosophical theories. Still, such theories help us provide a reasoned account of certain political beliefs.

Chapter Four

Theories of Health Justice

In an earlier chapter we have seen that health can be understood either as an element of well-being or as an asset. The latter idea, health as asset, interprets health as a means to pursue certain goals. The former, health as well-being, stresses the intrinsically valuable condition of being healthy. Health itself can be defined in negative terms, as absence of disease, and positively, as an ideal of organismic functioning. This has repercussions how theories might address the relevant topic of health justice. We end up with four different focal points of health justice: (1) illness as negative impact on well-being, (2) positive health as element of well-being, (3) disease as preventing opportunities and (4) positive health as advantage.

The first focal point leads to a theory of health justice that aims to tackle ill health. It is concerned with helping citizens deal with disease, either by curing it or by compensating for relevant impairments. The second focal point can in addition be concerned with the relative level of health—that is, whether people are less healthy than others. Seeing health as an asset—as an instrument to use when competing for other goods within society—either focuses on those health conditions that undermine the pursuit of normal opportunities, as in the third focal point, or aims at improving health to further improve the opportunity range of people.

The different focal points can be combined with different principles of justice. The main contenders we have explored in the previous chapter are egalitarianism and sufficientarianism. Egalitarianism necessarily works from the perspective of comparative justice: what is due to people depends on how others fare. Sufficientarianism puts forward an account of noncomparative justice. Here what is due to people depends on their characteristics and whether they fulfil relevant criteria that ensure access to goods, not on the position of others. In general, sufficientarianism lends itself more easily to the focal point of negative health, because it sets a threshold of what is enough. Different grades of health that come with a positive account of health usually go along with egalitarian theories of health justice. But this merely states a general tendency; we will see that things get more complicated, especially when introducing further issues of justice, such as fair rationing.

Although in most welfare states every citizen has access to health-care resources independent of their ability to pay, there are only few examples of completely equal and universal health-care systems. In many countries there are residents who do not have access to health care at all, most importantly illegal immigrants or, in some cases, refugees. In these cases health care is not universally accessible. In addition, almost all countries allow for unequal access to health care, usually via a system of additional individual payments or copayments. Finally, there are important determinants of individual health that can be privately purchased or at least influenced by private investments. Most importantly, the level of education but also access to recreational activities and clean environment indirectly make a statistically relevant contribution to people's health statuses. Hence health is at least partly a marketable good.

I have stressed in the previous chapter that health-care institutions provide for meeting certain risks of life. Welfare states are supposed to enable citizens to live independently. This aim involves a kind of insurance to support them in situations of reduced ability, such as disease. Ideally, health-care institutions guarantee that every citizen can live, as far as possible, a full and healthy life. Since disease can affect everyone, access to health-care resources should not be restricted but universally offered. For the time being, we assume that 'universal' coverage here means access for all citizens of a state. This is indeed a common way to use the term. In a later chapter, we will scrutinise whether health care should be offered globally—so, in a sense, really 'universally'.

In addition to the question of scope, there is a question of levels of such access. It seems intuitively unfair that some people have more and better access to health-care institutions and as a result have a better chance of living longer and healthier lives. However, inequalities in health are almost impossible to prevent, especially in liberal states that allow citizens to freely purchase goods offered on a market. Still, those health-care resources that are financed by welfare-state institutions, either through taxes or compulsory insurance premiums, are normally offered equally to all citizens. This is because of the basic equality of moral and political status of all citizens. As a matter of justice, quality of health care provided by social institutions must not depend on ability to pay.

In this respect health care does not seem to be different from other resources provided by welfare states, such as education or pensions. But access to health care is more heavily regulated. First of all, whether a specific person at a particular time should be granted access to publicly funded health-care resources depends on expert statements about their health status. As we have seen in an earlier chapter, access usually depends on a diagnosis of disease or a significant threat to health. Second, the specific type and amount of resources is also granted on account of expert judgements. Doctors and other experts determine what is required to meet the specific health need during a process called medical indication. For instance, whether a person with cancer is offered a newly available treatment or transferred to palliative care depends on the assessment of the patient's condition by medical personnel in relation to a complex mix of factual and normative assumptions. Importantly, what is granted to individual patients depends on external constraints—for instance, the budget of a particular unit of provision and the level of technical development and innovation. All these aspects make the public provision of health care rather special compared to other areas of the welfare state. The high value many people place on health in combination with the mentioned constraints unsurprisingly lead to social conflicts. Such a situation requires considerations of justice.

It should be obvious by now that it is notoriously unclear what justice in health care exactly requires. Even if we start from a fairly straightforward assumption that justice requires us to treat diseases, it is not clear at all what that means in terms of health-care resources. This is mainly because the means of meeting this goal can differ widely in terms of type and quality, whereas other traditional aims of welfare states, such as adequate education, housing or subsistence, allow for more or less determinate and standardised provision. In addition, individual health is influenced by an enormous number of factors. Occasionally, it might for instance be more effective in terms of addressing health problems to offer someone a socially engaging environment than to prescribe antidepressants. In other words, health-care provision is inextricably linked to many other areas of social and political concern and not restricted only to traditional medical institutions, such as hospitals and doctors' practices. When thinking about social justice in health care, it is therefore necessary to open the focus beyond what has traditionally been discussed under the rubric of justice in medicine.

It is also important to acknowledge that before any health-care resources, such as drugs or physiotherapies, can be allocated to patients, they have to be produced and financed. Medical personnel need to be educated, technology invented and developed, and knowledge about disease processes produced. All these pursuits are laborious and can be quite costly. To introduce a new drug, for instance, involves a large amount of research and testing, which is normally invested by pharmaceutical companies, not by state institutions. This connection of a vital aim of any welfare state—the health of citizens—with market-driven interests leads to a commodification of health care. Indeed, in many countries health is an economic enterprise served by marketable products as much as an individual concern addressed by medical institutions. As we will see in a later chapter, medicalisation and healthisation are outcomes of such developments.

To be sure, commodification does not have to be bad. For instance, it is doubtful whether a health-care system that is completely public and does not involve any private investments can be sustainable and technologically advanced. We cannot and need not discuss such complicated political and economic problems in this book. Suffice it to say that health care is not simply a public or communal concern.

Before we look more deeply into existing accounts of justice in health care, some distinctions between levels of allocation of resources should be introduced. These are common in the relevant literature. So far we have discussed justice as a problem located on what is usually called a macro level; it concerns the necessary investments of a society to provide a just level of health-care resources. In other words, the macro level addresses the budget that should be provided for health care. In contrast to this, issues of justice can also be discussed on a micro level. Occasionally, in medical practice decisions have to be made to allocate resources between individual people. Most significantly, any organ that is procured for transplantation can only be allocated to one person. This fact leads to conflicts of interests and requires considerations of justice. It should be clearly stated that we are here concerned with issues of social justice, not individual justice regarding, for instance, whom to treat first. Our main concern is located on the macro level. Still, when discussing rationing later in this chapter it will be seen that there are important considerations of social justice that apply within the constraints of a fixed budget.

Theories of social justice aim at enabling people to pursue relevant goals. They aim at enabling in contrast to implementing these goals because a relevant aspect of social justice is allowing people to make their own choices. Hence the focus is on the conditions that allow people to achieve the relevant goals if they want to. In a previous chapter, we identified two different general goals that are usually connected to health: well-being and opportunities. These two goals partly determine what kind of 'currency' theories of health justice endorse. Especially the notion of well-being can be fleshed out in many different ways and hence leads to variants of conceptions of health justice. The basic distinction between well-being and opportunities will structure the following sections. Yet it might be worth stressing that the distinction mainly serves analytic purposes. Theories of health justice often do not fall neatly into either camp.

HEALTH JUSTICE: PROMOTING WELL-BEING

Well-being is a term that needs to be explained. Most people would probably understand it to mean a positive feeling—something a person experiences as pleasant. But *well-being* can also refer to situations in which a person fares or lives well. This does not require pleasant experiences. Health, similarly, is not a condition we experience as such. Health is 'hidden' from us in the sense that we can only experience its lack in situations of illness. Health, in connection to well-being, is probably best conceived as the well functioning of an organism. So well-being should not be understood, for the purposes of our study, as requiring conscious experience. Certain conditions can enhance well-being without involving pleasure or similar mental states.

Perhaps because of these possible confusions due to the vague notion of well-being, many theorists rather use the term *capabilities*, although it means something similar. The concept of capabilities was originally developed by Amartya Sen, who used it to shape a theory of social justice based on this currency. Capabilities are effective freedoms to achieve valuable states of being and activity. Sen has called these 'doings' and 'beings' *functionings*, which admittedly might lead to confusion within the context of this study, as they are not the same as biological functions, which were discussed in an earlier chapter. Having capabilities enables people to lead valuable lives due to their own choices. In other words, the level or set of capabilities that is accessible to people reflects their 'freedom to choose from possible livings'[1].

Sen has stayed uncommitted regarding the substance of capabilities. Martha Nussbaum, in contrast, has developed a list of capabilities and hence decided on what valuable 'doings' and 'beings' for human beings are. She starts from a rich theory of human flourishing, which goes back to ancient philosophical ideas about the good life for human beings. What is good for human beings, in her account, is based on an interpretation of what kind of beings we are. Such a philosophical method, grounding an account of the good for human beings on assumptions about their nature, has been called essentialism. It should be said, however, that this very notion has led to some confusion, and Nussbaum has avoided the term in more recent publications. Setting the methodological concern aside for our purposes and returning to the issue of health justice, it should be noted that in Nussbaum's theory good health features as one of the central human capabilities.

The capabilities approach has been endorsed by numerous thinkers who have applied it more specifically to health justice. Interestingly, these theorists also expand the focus of social justice beyond the margins of medical care to issues of public health. Perhaps it is not a coincidence that they acknowledge the relevant connections between conditions of living and individual health, because they start from a broad conception of capabilities. According to this view, the good life of human beings consists of many and partially interlinked elements. Health is one important constituent of flourishing and health is partly determined by other capabilities.

Madison Powers and Ruth Faden, in their book *Social Justice: The Moral Foundations of Public Health and Health Policy*, explicitly avoid the terminology of capabilities, although they offer a similar theory. They directly focus on the notion of well-being, because they believe it is not adequate to drive a wedge between actual achievements of certain states and being enabled to achieve these, which is basically the idea of functionings versus capabilities. Especially for health, if it is a constitutive element of the good for human beings, it does not seem important whether bringing health about is based on using one's own freedom. 'Being healthy matters to our well-being whether or not that state is achieved by our action or by the action, say, of governmental bodies that secure for us potable water'[2]. Still, Powers and Faden acknowledge constraints on enforcing well-being by government action, so in the end the issue seems to be based purely on a conceptual preference. After all, Sen and other authors following his lead also intend to stress effective enablement as the goal of social justice. Some conditions of people need to be met and not merely made possible to enable citizens to live a decent life. For instance, a certain level of education seems to be required before certain freedoms can be reached at all. In other words, capabilities are founded on certain levels of functioning being achieved.

Powers and Faden list six essential dimensions of well-being: health, personal security, reasoning, respect, attachment and self-determination. In terms of the different theories of justice we have distinguished in the previous chapter, their theory of health justice should be categorised as a variant of sufficientarianism that also includes an element of relational egalitarianism. Importantly, their account connects the six dimensions in an overarching theory of health justice, as opposed to a theory of social justice that is restricted to the provision of medical resources. After all, as research into the social determinants of health has established, the mentioned dimensions all have an impact on the health of a population.

Although their theory is sufficientarian—that is, it aims to provide enough in terms of the dimensions of well-being—inequalities can have an indirect significance, as they might undermine a sufficient level, for instance, of respect. Also, economic inequalities in situations where some fail to reach the threshold might establish relevant information as to how a more just situation can be achieved. It might then be justifiable to reallocate economic resources in order to finance enough for all along the dimensions of well-being. Still, the primary normative focus in this theory is on providing a sufficient level of well-being to all citizens.

Jennifer Prah Ruger is explicitly committed to the capabilities framework. In her book *Health and Social Justice*[3], she specifically focuses on 'health capability'—people's capability of living a healthy life. In terms of social justice, her theory aims at a specific form of equality called shortfall equality. According to this idea, the actual achievement of health capability for different people needs to be assessed against a standard of an optimal average for this group. We have already seen that it is probably impossible to ever reach equality of health. However, people can be seen as having a particular level of maximal health that is possible for them. People with certain disabilities, for instance, will have a different maximal potential for health capability than will people without disabilities. Equality in terms of health capability will be reached if everyone has achieved the maximal level of health possible for them. Hence, this differs from a threshold notion of enough health, as in a sufficientarian approach. Altogether, Ruger's theory stands between a straightforward egalitarian and a sufficientarian point of view; it defies simple categorisation.

Sridhar Venkatapuram is another theorist who uses capabilities as a currency of justice. In contrast to the other authors discussed in this section, he thoroughly scrutinises the concept of health. For reasons laid out in the first chapters of this book, this seems to me to give Venkatapuram's approach an important advantage. It is important to be clear about the interpretation of the concept of health when discussing health justice. Health, for him, is the ability to achieve vital goals. This notion is strongly related to Nordenfelt's analysis, which was introduced in the second chapter. Importantly, health is not restricted to the absence of disease.

Venkatapuram uses Nussbaum's list of capabilities to flesh out the conception of vital goals, whose realisation is enabled when being healthy. This is important for issues of social justice, as the list of capabilities provides the currency of justice. Venkatapuram adds the original idea to see the capability of being healthy as a kind of overarching capability. Remember that health is influenced by numerous aspects of human life, such as feeling respected in society or having access to clean air or recreational facilities. Including these social determinants of health in a theory of health justice now leads to the thought that health can be 'conceived as a meta-capability, the capability to achieve a cluster of basic capabilities to be and to do things that reflect a life worthy of equal human dignity'[4].

Venkatapuram seems to opt for a sufficientarian approach, because he wants to include threshold levels of the basic capabilities, and altogether opts for a moral entitlement to reach a sufficient level of the capability to be healthy. However, he also adds—similar to Powers and Faden—that inequalities may lead to consequences that undermine some people's capabilities. Health inequalities, according to this thinking, are not intrinsically unjust but might be evidence of otherwise unjust conditions. Just think, by way of an example (my own) about the ostracising effect of having no teeth due to the significant costs of dental care in many countries. When we acknowledge the social determinants of health, we can see the connections between health and social inclusion more generally.

HEALTH JUSTICE: PROMOTING OPPORTUNITIES

Although capabilities can also be seen in relation to opportunities—after all, they are stating specific effective freedoms of people—the idea of health justice as promoting opportunities can be distinguished. Here the focus is not on what being able to do certain things means for a person's well-being. Rather, the idea of opportunities pertains to having relevant options. It is about open doors, so to speak—hence about the external, not internal, conditions of persons. Having opportunities, in the perspective taken here, is what has earlier been called an asset. This includes the interpersonal aspect of possibly having an advantage over others. Accordingly, health is mainly understood as a means to pursue opportunities and not as an end in its own right.

The most prominent theory of health justice in this perspective stems from Norman Daniels. Initially in his book *Just Health Care* Daniels discussed health care with a focus on medical resources[5]. In his more recent work, specifically in his book *Just Health*, he has expanded his focus to include the social determinants of health within a broad theory of health justice. Health, for him, is discussed within the framework set by social primary goods, which Rawls developed as a currency—or metric—of justice. Although Daniels does not introduce health as a social primary good in its own right, it is for him a means to maintain such basic resources. Therefore, health-care institutions are required for achieving social justice. Social primary goods, for Rawls and Daniels, are all-purpose means that can be used for any life plan. Every person, therefore, has an interest in them. Rawls never discussed health and health care thoroughly; Daniels's theory can be interpreted as a Rawlsian theory within the area of health justice. We have already seen in the previous chapter that Rawls's theory broadly falls into the egalitarian camp, Daniels's theory can also be deemed egalitarian, because he defends health care as a means to fair equality of opportunity.

Interestingly, Daniels includes an explicit conception of the basic notions of health and disease. He interprets health negatively—which has important repercussion we will discuss shortly—and disease for him is based on the naturalist analysis, which was already introduced in the first chapter of this study. For Daniels, health-care needs are constituted by cases of disease, not by instances of worse health over and above the threshold of negative health—that is, the absence of disease. So, in a much-discussed example, Daniels would not see a health-care need involved in the case of a child whose parents are very small in contrast to a child who suffers from growth hormone deficiency, even though their predicted height without growth hormone treatment would be the same. Despite this restriction to disease, Daniels accounts for health risks and accordingly for preventive measures in his theory of social justice via the known determinants of health. It is not just the presence but also the threat of disease that is relevant from his perspective of social justice.

Disease for Daniels is normatively significant as a matter of justice because it undermines the normal opportunity range of people. Not all cases of disease, understood as impairments of normal organismic functioning, actually do reduce the opportunity range of people, and hence not all diseases are worthy of publicly funded treatment. As mentioned, the framework of opportunities brings Daniels in close connection to egalitarian theories of justice. The main purpose of health care seems to be to level the playing field when pursuing a life plan. But Daniels's theory does not clearly fall into the egalitarian camp. After all, his theory of health justice aims at securing a normal opportunity range for everyone; the notion of normality seems to set a noncomparative standard. In addition, the theory addresses diseases and related risks only, not any other health inequalities, such as comparatively lower fitness or nonpathological disadvantages.

A straightforwardly luck-egalitarian theory of health justice has been put forward by Shlomi Segall. He opts for a principle of justice that requires an equal opportunity for everyone to be 'as healthy as possible'[6]. Intuitively, it seems indeed unfair if people suffer disadvantages that are caused by factors beyond their control. Being in worse health than others is a variant of such unfair disadvantages.

The flip side of such an approach is of course the need to establish an assessment of individual responsibility for health status to determine whether a health disadvantage is actually unfair. This is a difficult task, as we will see in a later section of this chapter. Nonetheless, there are quite sophisticated approaches to solve this very problem, most importantly by the economist John Roemer, who has developed a scheme for measuring effort and applied it, by way of example, to the case of smoking as a cause for health needs, more specifically lung cancer treatment.

Still, to let down people who have fallen ill and as a result are in need—perhaps even in need of life-saving treatment—only because they are held responsible for their condition seems an unacceptable consequence of luck egalitarianism. Should we really let people suffer or even die, although they could be saved, because they chose imprudently? On the other hand, asking people to take responsibility for their choices, at least in cases where health risks are known, seems to be a matter of respect. In addition, people would still be able to purchase required treatment out of their own pockets. Alternatively, higher insurance premiums or special taxes for health-risky lifestyles could be introduced. But be that as it may, there will probably always be some patients without the necessary private funds; compulsory additional schemes seem to come with unfair consequences, as they are based on ability to pay. It seems accordingly more sensible to at least offer basic health care to everyone and introduce considerations of responsibility at a less basic level of health care. In other words, a combination of equality of opportunity for health with a sufficiency baseline seems a better option. Segall opts for this solution, though it should be added that he regards the reasons for an unconditional basic package of health care to be grounded in other considerations than the ones put forward by the principle of equality of opportunity for health. Altogether, his account of health justice is, therefore, pluralist.

AGGREGATION AND RATIONING

So far, our considerations about health justice have been largely concerned with the grounds of justified claims and with the social conditions that ought to be achieved as a matter of justice. Most theories of health justice, despite their differences, aim at assessing the social conditions in which citizens are enabled to live a healthy life of their own. However, the means in order to reach this aim are limited. Therefore, we usually include the disclaimer 'as much as possible' in the formulation about the aim of health justice. The notion of what is possible, however, is vague: it may refer to factual feasibility or to what is reasonable. It seems that welfare states can always do more to improve the capability to be healthy or the range of opportunities of their citizens. But states' resources, usually drawn from taxes, are restricted, and health care competes with other areas of provision, such as education, culture or public transport. Hence it is advisable to think about a prudent way to use the available financial resources effectively and efficiently. Occasionally representatives of institutions and politicians need to make difficult decisions about alternative possible health policies or treatment options. After all, very often societies cannot do all that would actually be doable—or, rather, they deem it imprudent. In summary, the apparently straightforward disclaimer 'as much as possible' is not so much concerned with medical feasibility, regarding technology and the like, as it is concerned with the value society places on health in relation to other important values, which is a far more complicated and normatively loaded matter.

Ethical deliberation about priorities is usually supported by a process called *aggregation*. Aggregation weighs different normatively relevant considerations—such as costs of an option or the amount of suffering prevented—in order to reach a conclusive decision about the best possible decision between alternatives. If such a decision involves the rejection of a specific treatment option from the bundle of publicly funded health-care resources, then this is regularly called *rationing*. Although a claim to publicly funded treatment might generally be acknowledged, because there is a real health need, the specific aim might nevertheless be seen as less important than others or the means to achieve it as too expensive, given the available resources. To give an example: A disease such as cancer is certainly acknowledged as justifying claims to health-care resources. However, this alone does not establish an entitlement to any available treatment.

The very fact that public funds to finance health care are limited leads some thinkers to claim that rationing is also inevitable. This assertion, however, is based on equating the notion of the limitation of resources, which is a descriptive concept, with the normative concept of scarcity. It has already been established in the previous chapter that the scarcity of health-care resources cannot be seen as a straightforward fact, because it is relative to the extent of justified claims—which means that there might actually be more than enough health-care resources available. Rationing might therefore not be necessary, either. A justified decision to decline a possible treatment by public funds is not properly called rationing; rather, it amounts to reasonably denying an entitlement. To determine entitlements, after all, means to flesh out a conception of social justice. Aiming at social justice does not mean backpedalling from maximal demands on account of limited resources. To be sure, whenever citizens are told that anything that can be done in terms of health care will actually be provided for, they will of course consider any restriction to the best possible public-health services as instances of rationing—as something taken away from them. But it seems obvious to me that such a judgement is based on conceptual confusion and unreasonable political promises.

There is a need to discuss the relative importance of health in contrast to other aims of state action; and this might lead to reasons to restrict, say, the provision for the capability to be healthy. As mentioned, we have so far looked into the normative foundations of public provision for health, and hence into the justification for a state's health-care budget. A budget needs to be assessed in relation to other political aims. Such a task requires societal and political value judgements, which cannot be left only to a theory of justice. However, considerations of justice, including efficiency and relative economic worth of policies, can inform public deliberation and political decision. As I have said, the process and outcome of such debates is often, slightly misleadingly, collected under the rubric of rationing. Another common term for the same process, *prioritising*, is also misleading, because it suggests that nonprioritised treatment is merely postponed, whereas in reality it will not be offered at all.

Most theorists probably agree that decisions to not offer—or, conversely, to prefer—specific medical treatments or public-health measures should be based on aggregation. This would involve some estimation as to how much health gain different options promise to achieve. But measurements about health are fairly complicated, to say the least. We have already seen in an earlier chapter that measurement of health status seems to be a hopeless task, because overall health involves so many different factors. Still, it is vital to make informed comparative decisions about the value of policies and treatment options. Hence there need to be criteria and standards that can be used for aggregation, even though they might only lead to proxies for health status. In health-care economics, several such standards have been introduced. They do not, strictly speaking, measure health itself but, rather, the value of health-related conditions.

A well-known measure is called quality-adjusted life year. QALY, as it is known, combines well-being-related assessment with statistical data regarding specific treatment options' influence on mortality rates. QALYs are basically an attempt to produce a quantifiable standard that is applied to different treatment options in order to make them comparable. Two different options might lead to a different amount of QALYs. In addition, the costs of the different treatments can be introduced and the respective ratio—cost QALYs—calculated. This is an exercise in cost-effectiveness analysis. It can be used in different ways—for instance, to compare a newly available treatment to an established option. More controversially, it can also be used to set absolute limits to possible treatments. If an available treatment is deemed to promise insufficient of QALYs or is not deemed cost-effective, the treatment might be taken out of the publicly funded health-care package because it does not provide—as it is put these days—'value for money'.

Given the controversy about restrictions in the provision of health care, it is not surprising that ethical concerns have been raised regarding the use of aggregation in political decision making. It seems to result in decisions that disadvantage some people just because they happen to have rare or severe diseases, where treatment is often very expensive. Aggregation might also lead to discrimination of some groups of people who might not benefit much from treatment because their quality of life even with treatment is deemed to be too low. This might be the case for people with disabilities.

Partly the problems mentioned are due to the measures, such as QALY, themselves. It is obviously a difficult task to determine the value of different health conditions. Usually the assessment is based on subjective rankings of real people, who fill in questionnaires. But it seems difficult to assess, say, the predicted quality of life of having to live with a catheter or after losing a leg. Especially regarding certain disabilities, there are common misperceptions regarding their impact on quality of life. In addition, even if improved and interpersonally valid measures could be developed, there is still the problem of not caring for patients only because their treatment is deemed too expensive in absolute terms or deemed insufficiently cost-effective. Morally speaking, this should not make a difference, one might think; we have a duty to rescue everyone we can, whatever the costs. Surely, there must be limits to aggregation.

However, it has already been established that effectiveness and efficiency are themselves normative considerations that should have an impact on decisions in situations of scarcity. Once we as a political community have made a decision to restrict funds for health care, we should spend the money in a reasonable way. In addition, political decisions are usually not, and should not be, driven merely by cost-effectiveness. There are other values that are put into the equation—for instance, whether the treatment under consideration is to the benefit of a vulnerable or generally disadvantaged group. Altogether, cost-effectiveness analysis is an indispensable element of determining health-care budgets, although its methodology might be improved, of course.

In addition to economic considerations, there are also attempts to use criteria to restrict budgets that have a more direct ethical significance. These can be either substantive or procedural. Criteria that have often been put forward are patient age and individual responsibility for health status. Procedural considerations concern the process of deliberating about restrictions, which is, in reality, a political practice.

When following a methodology of 'what the people think', substantive and procedural aspects can be linked. These days public participation in certain policy decisions has become an important element of political deliberation. For instance, citizen panels or other forms of 'mini-publics' have been established in numerous countries. In terms of theory, how to engage the public in the right way is itself a complicated methodological problem that cannot be tackled here. Suffice it to say that it is not merely about asking people what they prefer. The posed problem is, rather, what people think justice requires. In terms of the two mentioned criteria, age and responsibility, public opinion seems to be undecided. Especially when considering cultural differences, which are common in modern, multicultural societies, this might not be surprising.

Alternatively, theorists opt for a constructivist approach and introduce an idealised-choice situation—for instance, a prudent hypothetical insurer who needs to make a decision about the level of health-care provision for different phases of her life. In such an approach it is often claimed that justice would actually require a preference for spending more on health needs in earlier phases of life and restricting the budget for use in later life. It is important to see that such considerations are really about an idealised choice that is used for purposes of determining principles of social justice, similarly to the 'original position' that Rawls developed in his theory of justice that was explained in the previous chapter. Accordingly, it is not a value judgement about the relative value of old people in comparison to young people. Whatever its methodological merits, therefore, it cannot be said that such an approach would necessarily lead to age discrimination, although it should be acknowledged that there can be concerns about the implicit assumptions of such modelling of the choice situation that will, after all, disadvantage some age groups.

INDIVIDUAL RESPONSIBILITY FOR HEALTH STATUS

We hold people responsible for their choices. If they squander their money, for instance, they cannot claim it back from others, even if they are severely disadvantaged as a result. If students are not well prepared for an essay, they will be held responsible for a bad mark or even a fail. Similarly, it seems sensible to hold people responsible for their health status. At least it seems fair to prioritise treatment of those patients who were simply victims of brute bad luck. It seems just to maintain that everyone should have a fair opportunity to live a healthy life but unjust to ignore their own voluntary choices. At least theoretically, individual responsibility for health looks like a promising criterion for restricting a health-care budget. But as we shall see, it is much harder to put this into practice. The main practical problem is conclusively establishing a sufficient causal influence of individual free choices on health status. As we will see, this undermines the notion of individual responsibility for health status from a retrospective point of view. There might still be prospective—that is, forward-looking—elements of responsibility to consider within a theory of health justice.

Responsibility for health is often discussed not so much as an issue of justice but as an important element of the good life of people. It is well known that we can influence our health status in many ways—for instance, by choosing a healthy diet or doing physical exercise. In this respect it is a matter of prudence to live a healthy life, because disease usually impairs well-being. To prevent suffering, one should follow advice for staying healthy. The discussion we are interested in at this point is different. It is not about self-inflicted harm as such but, rather, about the consequences of such harm to others. Health-care resources are required to meet health needs, and the relevant resources are publicly funded by taking money from many others. A more direct harm to others by imprudent choices might be that their own health-care need might not be met because scarce resources are needed for the imprudent person who might be held responsible for her needy situation. From this perspective, individual choices become a public concern—indeed, a matter of social justice. Unhealthy choices affect others by reducing the amount of available resources.

As we have seen when discussing the general idea of luck egalitarianism, we need to distinguish between disadvantages that are due to the choices of people and disadvantages that are based on the circumstances people find themselves in. People can be held responsible for their choices but not their circumstances. From this perspective, if people are responsible for a suffered disadvantage, they have forfeit their claim to compensation on account of public funds.

The problem in the context of health-care justice is to conclusively establish whether the health condition of an individual claimant has been caused by her choices. This seems an extremely difficult task. Even when dealing with directly harmful substances, such as poison, it is not always directly clear whether the substance alone has led to a pathological condition. Diseases are usually multicausal, and many of the determinants are part of a person's circumstances—for instance, their genetic makeup.

There are also problems when trying to establish the voluntariness of choices. Consider the usual example of smoking: People of course know these days that smoking is harmful. But they often start smoking because of peer pressure or cultural and social impregnation about normal behaviour. Very often smokers are young when they start the habit, and there are questions about the strength of will of young people in dealing with the circumstances in which they find themselves. Smoking is addictive, of course, and hence also later in life there are doubts about the voluntariness of relevant choices.

In addition, very often people do not know about the causal links of certain choices and health risks. It seems arbitrary to deny compensation only in those cases where we happen to have knowledge about the impact of choices. Indeed, scientific evidence for these connections seems to be changing all the time. The way we live our lives in modern societies changes all the time and may introduce new health risks. For instance, highly demanding and stressful jobs with no time for rest and recreation seem to raise the risk for certain mental disorders. If we, as a solidaristic and compassionate society maintaining welfare institutions to care for the sick, contemplate denying compensation for self-inflicted diseases, we should be aware that perhaps the powerful parties in the political system might simply penalise those lifestyles they deem less valuable. When considering the usual grounds for restrictions of health care due to individual responsibility, smoking and unhealthy lifestyle choices, one might get the sense that typical middle-class values are being promoted.

Altogether, there seem to be too many ethical and feasibility issues when considering responsibility for health status as a criterion to restricting access to publicly funded health care. However, we have so far only considered responsibility for the fact that someone has a health need. This is a matter of retrospective responsibility. Things might look different when we look forward, at what happens when a person has a disease and is in need of treatment. Patients can be held responsible for their part in recovering from a particular health-care need. Accordingly, in this perspective it is not the alleged fact that they have harmed others indirectly by their own free choices but that they have an influence on the eventual amount of such indirect harm to others for which they can be held responsible. In other words, we are dealing here with a potential duty of patients to participate willingly in their treatment. They might be held responsible for the trajectory of a disease process and the return to health; they are not held responsible for the presence of a disease.

Duties of patients to participate in their treatment are not an outlandish idea. Indeed, they have been discussed in connection to the specific social role of being a patient in the work of the famous medical sociologist Talcott Parsons, who writes, 'The acceptance of the role as a patient, that is, participation in interaction with the health care agency, may be said to impose a definite responsibility on the patient in working toward the common goals of the system as a whole'[7].

It needs to be stressed that this idea does not undermine the well-established right of the patient to reject treatment options. It does not require blind compliance with medical advice but a general commitment to returning to health, which lack is, after all, the reason the patient requires the use of health-care resources in the first place. Also, patient responsibility is only temporary; once health has been regained, patient commitments terminate.

When considering patients' duties from the perspective of health justice, it seems obvious that citizens have a legitimate interest in patient choices because being a patient implies the use of publicly funded resources. Given the scarcity of resources implies an obligation to use medical resources effectively, efficiently and fairly. Importantly, prospective responsibility does not raise the same ethical and feasibility issues that afflict the idea of retrospective responsibility for health conditions: The individual contribution to an illness trajectory is straightforward. Patients do not lack information regarding their potential contribution to the healing process; indeed, that is part of the usual consultation with health-care personnel. Patients can change their lifestyles. Even addictions can be tackled with the right help; there are 'no excuses'. In addition, prospective responsibility applies to each disease condition, so there is no issue of arbitrariness.

Altogether, the idea of prospective responsibility does not suffer from the same defects as retrospective responsibility and might well be used for considering how to restrict access to health-care resources as a matter of social justice. The general notion is also established in the common social role of the patient. However, the normative consequences of prospective responsibility still need to be explored in further detail, which cannot be done in these pages. Personally, I would be worried about the long-term social consequences when introducing individual responsibility into considerations of health justice, even in its prospective version. Although it has strong normative reasons in its favour, it seems to me to undermine the very idea of solidarity, which, after all, is the foundational value underlying welfare-state institutions. I would be worried if we lived in societies where fellow citizens considered others mainly as competitors for scarce resources who should be held responsible so that they were the least possible burden to others.

CONCLUSION

We have used the distinctions between negative and positive health as well as between well-being and opportunities, which were explored in earlier chapters, to devise different focal points of theories of health justice. Health-care institutions are elements of welfare states; these usually aim at protecting citizens from certain common life risks. Ill health is one such risk. It should be clear by now that different theories of health justice vary in their assessment of what ill health means and what it implies in terms of justified claims of justice. Different existing theories of health justice can be mapped onto the aforementioned focal points. We have explored several such theories, though there are certainly more available in the relevant literature. Egalitarian theories tend to be in the camp promoting opportunities, whereas sufficientarian approaches lean towards promoting well-being. Such allocations of theories to focal points of course mainly serve the purpose of providing a straightforward structure, which should only build a starting point for delving deeper into individual theories. This will be a task left to the interested reader.

In this chapter we have also explored the ideas of aggregation and rationing, including some of the common pitfalls when using these instruments. They are mainly justified on the basis of scarcity of resources. We have already highlighted, in the previous chapter, that the idea of scarcity as such is slippery and requires a considerable amount of normative considerations. It should not be simply stated as a fact. Still, in reality there clearly is a need to restrict access to health-care resources to maintain viable and sustainable institutions. We have finally looked more closely into the notion of responsibility for health, because it seems to be a valid idea to hold people responsible for their own choices, even if these lead to disadvantages. I have argued that retrospective responsibility does not work well for concerns of health justice. However, prospective responsibility is an underexplored alternative, and I have hinted at some ways this idea might be fleshed out more thoroughly.

Chapter Five

Global Health Justice

So far we have discussed health justice within the borders of nation-states. Indeed, most health-care institutions and public-health instruments, such as hospitals, nursing homes or provision of clean water, operate in specific welfare states and are funded by citizens of these states. However, health is obviously a global concern of all human beings; it does not stop at borders. Some institutions already cater for health globally—most important among them the World Health Organization. There are also numerous charities and nongovernmental organisations that provide for health-care needs internationally. Their mission is usually not seen as a matter of justice but of charity. Yet it seems obvious that all human beings should have access to some level of health-care provision, since morally speaking all human beings are equal. If states cannot provide for the most basic health needs of their citizens, other states ought to help. At least, this is what seems to follow when we conceive of justice globally.

In this chapter we will look into the discussion of global health justice. We will scrutinise the reasons provided for a human right to health-care provision and what such a right might imply. More specifically, we will consider whether global health egalitarianism is a convincing theory. We will also examine what justice requires for noncitizens living within the borders of a state, especially refugees.

COSMOPOLITANISM

John Rawls was one of the first recent theorists of justice to consider issues of justice beyond the borders of states. His theory of justice was initially conceptualised for societies where citizens share a relationship of social cooperation and accordingly divide the resulting advantages between them.

This is founded on the basic moral idea of reciprocity. Rawls later developed a theory of a law of peoples, which, however, was conceptualised as a theory of justice between states. In congruence with the initial hypothetical and idealised-choice situation described in his theory of justice, where domestic principles of justice are determined, representatives are supposed to choose principles that regulate justice between states. In other words, Rawls's later account is a theory of international justice, not of global justice. Still, his law of peoples included a duty of states to support other states in situations of crisis, especially when conditions might undermine the maintenance of decent political and social institutions within a burdened state. Failure to provide basic health care might indeed lead to other states' being obligated to take over responsibilities. However, Rawls's theory of international justice is explicitly not egalitarian; he merely considers provision for basic needs, which is conceived as protection of human rights.

Critics pointed out that Rawls does not appreciate the interdependence of states in a globalised economy. Relevant advantages of social cooperation within nations-states are at least partly based on historical injustices—most importantly, on colonial exploitation. Competitive advantages are used to maintain exploitative circumstances. In addition, from a moral point of view it seems unjust that some states are better-off because they have access to valuable natural resources, such as crude oil or fertile soil. The Earth and its resources seem to have originally belonged to all human beings together—at least, this is what many cosmopolitans assume. It therefore seems unjustifiable to claim ownership without compensating for the resulting undeserved disadvantages of others. After all, natural resources are limited and cannot be appropriated without loss to others.

As regards theories of justice, the alternative to Rawls begins from the idea of basic moral equality of all human beings. National borders, from this point of view, are morally arbitrary. The idea of an initial-choice situation, where people consider principles of justice, is then not restricted to members of a specific society but applies directly to humanity. There is only one choice situation for determining principles of justice, not two, as in Rawls's thinking. Accordingly, a form of global egalitarianism is the outcome. Such an egalitarian outcome, it should be said, can also be reached by other methodologies than the Rawlsian one, which devises a contract theory, aiming at universal consent in a hypothetical-choice situation. Utilitarian thinkers also argue against the moral relevance of relational or geographic proximity.

The basic assumption to see individuals, not states, as the most basic normative unit of a theory of justice is called *cosmopolitanism*. It is contrasted with *statism*, a theory that assumes a stronger normative significance of national borders. Cosmopolitanism is also opposed to *nationalism*, which identifies a special moral relevance in relationships between conationals. These labels, as always, are to be understood as handy identifiers for theories that share specific basic premises. It should be said that there are numerous variations of theories that combine elements of different isms.

Cosmopolitans need not necessarily opt for a world state. Potentially, global institutions with coercive power over all citizens of the world would be a dangerous idea. Such amassing of power can be avoided by using a principle of subsidiarity, where domestic institutions deal with issues of justice and where sovereignty on a larger scale is only exercised in cases where the more local institutions fail. Within such a cosmopolitan framework, national states can justifiably exist. Still, moral duties of justice apply globally. Every human being owes something to everyone, even distant strangers. Consequently, the scope of justice within cosmopolitan thinking is wide, but there can be moderate versions of cosmopolitanism where universal duties of social justice are combined with an acknowledgement of special ties between people living in the same country or sharing a national identity.

Moderate versions of cosmopolitanism as well as versions of statism and nationalism share the idea that special relationships between people exist and justify different principles of justice for members of specific groups in contrast to global justice. It is not the arbitrary fact of having been born in a specific country or of being a member of a specific nation that has normative significance but the idea of belonging to a form of an ongoing joint political project. Although the idea of a nation is a historical construction, there are nevertheless manifest relationships within the citizenry of states. These are fluctuating relationships, of course, since the population in modern societies is constantly changing. Still, human beings generally show a sense of belonging to a specific country that has normative significance and cannot be simply brushed aside. This fact is important for the discussion about egalitarianism. Even egalitarian theories of justice are not necessarily egalitarian on a global scale. Egalitarian theories of justice, accordingly, might share a similar conception of global justice with nonegalitarian ones. In brief, the common denominator between all theories of global justice seems to be that every human being should be enabled to live at least a minimally decent life. We will now examine what this might mean in terms of health.

A HUMAN RIGHT TO HEALTH?

Normative thinking about justice is concerned with what the world should look like or, rather, what entitlements of people should be acknowledged or, in other words, which of their claims are justified. A normative perspective is different from a descriptive one, where we consider what entitlements people actually have. It is nevertheless illuminating to start our considerations regarding claims of global health justice by quoting from the Universal Declaration of Human Rights, adopted by the United Nations in 1948. After all, despite its lack of coercive power, the declaration, ratified by a huge number of countries, does have normative significance from the perspective of theorising within the methodology of 'what the people think'.

The first paragraph of article 25 reads, 'Everyone has the right to a standard of living adequate for the health and well-being of himself and of his family, including food, clothing, housing and medical care and necessary social services, and the right to security in the event of unemployment, sickness, disability, widowhood, old age or other lack of livelihood in circumstances beyond his control'[1]. The formulation is not specific as to what a standard of living 'adequate' for individual health would be. This is apparently considered to be relative to circumstances. Interestingly, the link to social determinants of health, such as housing, is highlighted. A human right to health according to this perspective includes more than simply the provision of medical resources.

The World Health Organization, in the preamble of their constitution, similarly focus on a human right to health. The constitution was signed in 1946 and enacted in 1948, the same year that the Universal Declaration of Human Rights was enacted, which perhaps underscores the historical context, during which time the world was coming to terms with the atrocities of the Second World War. The WHO constitution declares that 'the enjoyment of the highest attainable standard of health is one of the fundamental rights of every human being without distinction of race, religion, political belief, economic or social condition'[2].

This formulation sounds more ambitious, especially if we consider that the WHO defines *health* as 'a state of complete physical, mental and social well-being and not merely the absence of disease or infirmity'[3]. Accordingly, the human right to health, in this perspective, seems to demand achievement of the highest standard of complete well-being, which basically sounds like a right to perfect happiness. It is unlikely that such a right would be a reasonable aim of justice.

However, the WHO qualifies that it ought to be 'highest *attainable* standard of health' (emphasis mine). The International Covenant on Civil and Political Rights, another legal document relevant in this context, uses the same wording[4]. Now, we have seen in the previous chapter that it is common to qualify claims of justice relative to what is feasible in typical situations of scarcity. We have also seen that qualifying terms like *attainable*, *possible* or *feasible* require some interpretation. Hence it is actually not clear whether the WHO's ambition is really greater than the one we find in the Universal Declaration of Human Rights.

The WHO's qualification also seems to undermine the objection that the WHO's demand for the provision of happiness for all creates a 'bottomless pit' of resource demand. In addition, when considering once again the social determinants of health, we might even begin to see the WHO's definition of health in a different light: after all, a state of 'complete' well-being might well mean complete in the sense of including all aspects of health, not just the medical elements. This is different from a scalar notion of a highest level of well-being, which would indeed be a problematic aim of social or global justice.

Many theorists complain that the notion of a right to health does not make sense because we would not say that someone who falls ill has had her right violated. After all, disease is very often a natural process, and there is, then, nobody to blame for its presence. Claim rights imply duties of others to provide for and maintain the content of the right; in the relevant case, this means the duty to protect the health of others. Yet it seems wrong to say that people have violated their duty when someone falls ill.

This complaint is not adequate, however. Consider a similar right: We would not normally say that a person's right to life—which, most people agree, is an important human right—has been violated if a person falls down the stairs and breaks her neck. In general, many rights are such that the absence or loss of the good they secure does not automatically entail a rights violation. Accordingly, it is not the fact that someone has a disease that is relevant for a possible rights violation but whether she is supported in tackling the disease. In other words, we can say that the right to health is forward-looking in the sense that there are duties to enable people to get back to health in cases of illness. This interpretation might also imply rights violations in cases of preventable human-made threats to health—for instance, when health and safety regulations are ignored or when the environment is severely polluted.

Given the possible misunderstandings regarding a right to health, it might nevertheless be better to talk of a human right to have relevant health-care needs met. This would comprise preventive, curative and rehabilitative measures, including the social determinants of health. How far these measures would go—that is, exactly what the right to have one's health-care needs met encompasses—is still undecided. An important problem for theories of global health justice is, for instance, whether health inequalities between different nations are a matter of injustice. We will look into this problem regarding the content of the right to health in the next section.

The global right to health is considered to be a moral human right. It is already acknowledged as a legal right as well. It should be acknowledged, however, that a global right to health, as with other human rights, needs political enforcement in order to become 'real'. Some theorists are worried that a right that is not maintained by global governance undermines the very idea of justice. A basic moral principle is that we can only be obliged to do what is possible for us: 'Ought implies can'. As long as people cannot provide for the global right to health to become real, due to lack of required institutions of governance, it seems wrong to say they have to fulfil a corresponding duty. However, it seems clear that, again, what is possible can be understood in many different ways. To provide for a moral right to health might be impossible today, but perhaps not tomorrow. Certainly, issues of justice cannot be wholly determined under assumptions of nonideal circumstances. Without any aspiration to change societies and institutions, the very idea of justice loses its moral bite.

GLOBAL HEALTH INEQUALITIES

Health-related indicators, especially life expectancy, show worldwide variation on a large scale. To take just two random examples: The average life expectancy in Nigeria in 2016 was 55.2 years, according to data retrieved from the WHO website[5]. In contrast, that same year people in Bahrain could expect to live 79.1 years. It is very unlikely that the lower life expectancy of Nigerian citizens comes down to their own voluntary choices. It seems pretty obvious that their disadvantages are undeserved and that they are very likely to be explained by the circumstances in which they live. Statistical data on earlier deaths in a population might be explainable by violent conflicts, higher suicide rates, low standards in road safety, pollution, restricted access to nutritious food or clean water and so on. It is extremely unlikely that anyone would choose to live in such conditions.

There might, however, be a reason to hold Nigerians, or any other people who have a lower life expectancy, responsible for the situation, because these states usually determine their own political destiny. We should, in a word, acknowledge national self-determination. Such an argument puts personal and national autonomy in parallel and sees similar ethical norms in place. We allow individuals to make their own choices, and we usually do not believe they have a claim for compensation if they suffer disadvantages as a result.

This argument will not take us very far. It might be used to justify differences in life expectancy between, say, Chile (79.5 in 2016) and the United States (78.5 in 2016)[6], because the differences here might well be explainable by different policies—for instance, different levels of investment in public-health measures. But it is implausible to say that Nigeria's considerably lower life expectancy can entirely be explained by Nigerians' merely having made imprudent political choices for which they should be held responsible. In addition, we have already seen in the previous chapter that retrospective responsibility is not a useful notion for consideration of health justice. Even on an individual level it is an impossible task to determine whether a specific health condition has been caused by choices or circumstances. It will always be a mix of both, and hence we cannot hold people responsible for the causation of disease. It will be even harder to make the idea of holding people responsible work on a national level. Finally, there can be doubts about jointly holding all citizens responsible for collective decisions. Even in democratic countries there is no real joint choice of citizens that determines the alleged will of the people. There will always be some people who oppose particular political decisions of the government. It might therefore be wrong to collectively hold citizens of the relevant country responsible for severely harmful choices—at least, not without additional argument—even if we were able to solve the problem of disentangling causal factors.

In summary, the issue of national self-determination does not seem to be at the heart of normative concerns when discussing extreme global health inequalities. Inequality in life expectancy as such, however, does not seem to amount to injustice. Inequality might be an indicator of unjust circumstances, but to diagnose injustices certainly requires further analysis of the statistical data and the relevant causal factors. Life expectancy is merely a crude proxy for health differences between populations anyway. It is doubtful whether such a measure has direct normative significance beyond its rhetorical force.

Although there are doubts about straightforwardly using statistical data about inequality in health-related measures, it is obvious that differences between countries might be evidence of underlying injustices, especially when they are as staggering as between Nigeria and Bahrain. We just said that further analysis is needed to make better normative use of the epidemiological findings. In public health, one such analysis has become very influential. Margaret Whitehead suggests that health disparities are unjust—or amount to *inequities*, to use the preferred term in many social sciences—when they are avoidable, unnecessary and unfair[7]. Unfairness is further analysed in relation to the causation of different health statuses. This approach does not differ significantly from the perspective of normative analysis in many theories of justice. The main practical problem, then, is to better distinguish between choices and circumstances as possible causes of health inequalities. Whitehead's suggestions have led to methodological improvements, although it is surely an ongoing effort to improve the science of social epidemiology.

To see health-related disparities as potential evidence of injustice, not as directly wrong in terms of justice, helps to see the connection of health justice to other aspects of social justice. If people die prematurely or populations show unusually high levels of morbidity, there might be underlying causes, such as gender discrimination or oppression, that can explain these inequalities. Interestingly, the normative reasons why these underlying structures should be deemed unjust are themselves connected to their impact on health. In other words, certain social conditions can be deemed unjust partly because they undermine an important individual and social value: health.

In terms of global health inequities, such a result of normative analysis—diagnosing an injustice—leads to further problems that go far beyond the remit of this study. For instance, it might be asked whether there is a duty to intervene politically in countries that are deeply unjust. What is more, a change in social conditions might require significant changes in traditional cultural practices. Again, it is not clear whether such changes are justified. To give an example: Effective malaria protection requires the use of mosquito nets, but cultural beliefs might prevent people from using these nets. In one actual case, the netting was considered too similar to fabric used to bury the dead. Does a duty of justice to help other people to have their health needs met merely demand that access to mosquito nets and information regarding their use be provided, or should cultural beliefs that prevent people from taking preventive care be deemed types of circumstantial injustices that need to be altered as well?

In summary, global health inequalities certainly raise concerns of justice. However, it needs to be acknowledged that normative analysis relies on epidemiological data that necessarily use proxies for health statuses, since health itself cannot be measured. In addition, there are intricate problems to be solved surrounding the basic distinction between choice and circumstances. These are partly to do with the science of epidemiology but are also normative. After all, there are reasons to doubt the normative significance of the very distinction between choice and circumstances when it comes to considerations of health justice.

It is very unlikely that decisions about the content of global health-care provision can be based on theoretical considerations only. This has been stressed before, and the same line of thinking applies also to the issue of global health justice. Determining a just 'package' of health-care treatments and provisions requires political processes that involve public deliberation. Still, theoretical considerations regarding the notions of health and disease and concerning different theories of social justice can provide reasons in such deliberation. In the final chapters we will see how further analyses regarding the goals of medicine and the concept of need can inform public debate.

HEALTH JUSTICE FOR NONCITIZENS

Global justice is not only a matter of rights of human beings who live in other countries. It is also a concern regarding the justified claims of people who currently reside in a particular country that is not their country of origin. This has become a far greater concern than in the past, especially since the emergence of the so-called refugee crisis. Questions concerning health justice for noncitizens are even more difficult to handle for theories of social justice than—for lack of a better descriptor—external global justice. They are more difficult because we need an account of the moral and political status of noncitizens before discussing the justified claims of noncitizens. Not surprisingly, this is highly contested territory. Accordingly, no straightforward answer regarding health justice for noncitizens can be expected.

The emerging scholarly literature on—what could be called—domestic global justice has been largely concerned with political rights of refugees and migrants. Very little has been published from a normative point of view on health justice for resident aliens. This makes the following paragraphs an attempt to explore a relatively uncharted territory.

The demands of global justice applied within states do not straightforwardly seem to allow for differential treatment of residents, whatever their origin. Many theories of global health justice allow for different levels of provision, as long as a basic minimum is guaranteed everywhere. The rationale for different levels of health provision usually refers to the significance of relative levels of development in different countries and to the moral importance of national self-determination. But these aspects do not appear in the cases we are considering now. To only provide health care on the level we find in, say, Somalia for refugees who arrive in Norway seems unjustifiable. Yet opting for equal treatment of all people currently residing within a country might lead to the justification of a significant volume of additional claims within specific countries, especially within those that take large numbers of refugees and immigrants. This assertion, which is an empirical claim, should, however, immediately be qualified, since findings suggest that the health status of migrants is generally quite high. The situation for refugees might of course be different, because they often have experienced enormous hardship and suffering.

Normatively speaking, adding to the problem of additional pressure on the domestic health-care budget is that especially refugees and asylum seekers in many countries are not allowed to work, which means they cannot contribute to the production of public funds for health care via insurance premiums, taxes or directly by doing health-care work themselves. Migration and refugee movements have raised lots of concerns in many countries; whether these are reasonable is not for me to discuss here. For instance, worries regarding the possible additional pressure on the National Health Service by incoming citizens from other European Union countries, who would have the same entitlement to use it 'free at point of service', influenced public opinion in the United Kingdom.

In reality, at least some groups of resident aliens usually do not have the same entitlement as local citizens. In Germany, for example, refugees and asylum seekers receive medical treatment in cases of emergency and acute disease, but they have no entitlement to other health-care resources that are available to German and other European citizens. Such unequal access to health care within a country seems to many people to be based on morally arbitrary factors—basically, on having a suitable passport or not.

As has been said before, no specific content of provision of health care can be shown to be required as a matter of justice. Although we can agree that all health-care needs should be addressed, this does not imply a particular package of health-care resources. Cancer, for example, can be treated with an array of highly advanced technologies and drugs, but it can also be treated by providing pain relief and applying palliative care. In other words, theories of justice might agree on the just causes of treatment, but they do not necessarily agree on the required just means of treatment.

The problems in determining a specific content of the right to have one's health needs met should nevertheless not ease all worries about the differential treatment of noncitizens in many countries. It might actually appear obvious that they are discriminated against because they are treated differently on the mere grounds of having a different nationality—or, in other senses, of 'not belonging' to the domestic society. That the lack of citizenship might be deemed a morally arbitrary factor, similar to sex, race, disability or age, preventing resident noncitizens from getting the same package of health care—including public-health measures regarding the social determinants of health—seems to constitute an unfair disadvantage. In this perspective, the injustice is not so much the absolute level of provision provided refugees and other groups but their relative level in contrast to compatriots. In other words, it is the unequal treatment that raises moral concerns.

However, it should be noted that almost all countries allow for differences in levels of access to health care and social determinants of health for their citizens. Citizens may opt for additional health insurance, or they can live in areas with healthier conditions. People are allowed, as it were, to convert their higher income or higher level of education into measures that can improve their health. Hence, inequality in accessing health-care institutions as such does not seem to raise moral concerns with many people. It would be different, of course, were noncitizens not to have access at all to health-care institutions, but this is not the case.

The main normative notions that need consideration here are discrimination and equal access. Equal access is not simply meant in the sense of being equal in having access to health-care institutions or in not being excluded from access. Rather, when it is said that equal access should be provided, the notion is meant in a comparative way: the same level of provision is supposed to be required for compatriots and noncompatriots.

Discrimination against someone is a form of injustice or moral wrong. It consists of treating someone differently without having a convincing reason to do so. Discrimination in the moral sense consists of arbitrarily treating someone differently than another. Usually this happens when irrelevant group membership is used as a basis of disadvantaging people. Hence it is not merely the fact that someone, or a group, is treated differently than others that makes an action or a policy wrong but that there is no plausible normative rationale for it. Belonging to a different sex or having a disability are not considered plausible reasons for treating people differently in accessing health-care institutions. However, being a noncitizen might well be a plausible basis for differential treatment. Accordingly, preventing noncompatriots from accessing certain health-care resources is not necessarily a form of discriminatory practice. Whether lack of citizenship is a good reason for differential treatment depends on how we should normatively conceive of health-care institutions and welfare institutions more generally. On the one hand, it seems obvious that a state, for instance, has a duty to provide health and safety policies for all workers and that it would discriminate against working immigrants if it would only secure a lower level of health and safety regulations for them. Some welfare institutions and provision of public goods are grounded in individual duties that are transferred to the state for reasons of moral division of labour.

On the other hand, we are now considering a situation where an existing harm—a disease—needs to be removed or compensated for, not merely prevented. The relevant situation is normatively different because the duty to alleviate harm to others does not have a clear-cut addressee and no straightforward content, either. In terms of the case we are discussing now, it would seem adequate to maintain that the health-care needs of citizens should be seen to by their compatriots. This is because they share a relationship of reciprocity, where everyone helps the other, so that all benefit jointly. Provision of health care is here assumed to be based on associative duties—obligations people have because they belong to a group that shares certain interests and jointly maintains specific institutions. Consequently, it seems that the fitting addressee of the duty to help noncitizens residing in a different country would be their own compatriots. If this cannot be achieved for any reason, citizens of the host country take over the duty, because harm triggers the duty to help for those who are in a position to help. Accordingly, it would be a form of discriminating against noncitizens if they were offered no health care provision whatsoever.

Still, it is not clear why noncompatriots should be owed the same level and kind of provision as compatriots. Importantly, helping people in need and alleviating harm can be done in many different ways. For instance, pain can be treated by applying analgesics or by providing physiotherapy sessions. The exact level of provision by welfare-state institutions to meet harm depends on domestic political decisions. Whereas the reason for providing basic access to health-care institutions grounds on considerations of justice, the concrete level of health-care provision within a country is not determined by principles of justice alone. Decisions about the health-care budget relative to other national expenses are based on political considerations as to how valuable health is to the citizenry. It would, similarly, require a political decision to expand the same level of health-care provision to noncitizens.

Such a decision would be a collective normative statement as to how valuable the health of noncompatriots is to the host nation. In this connection it would indeed be nice to see a greater amount of solidarity with vulnerable groups, especially refugees, in affluent countries. In reality, the alleged burden of catering for more people due to the refugee 'crisis' has led to a widespread mood in favour of restricting the level of health care for noncitizens. As I have said, I do not believe that this practice is unjust as such, but it seems in other ways normatively problematic, mainly because of the 'message' sent to migrants and refugees.

In summary, I have been arguing for an account of global health justice that can be described as sufficientarian. According to the solution developed in this chapter, it would constitute a form of discrimination against noncitizens residing in a country—for instance, migrants and refugees—if they were offered no health care at all. Still, this does not imply that the same level of health care needs to be provided for all people residing in a country as a matter of justice. There are numerous normative reasons to do so, of course—for instance, to prevent the impression of allowing second-class treatment or to secure a sense of belonging in new members of society. But I do not believe there is a right of noncitizens to have their health needs met in the same way as compatriots' needs are met, mainly because I believe compatriots develop an association including relevant duties of solidarity that go over and above what 'we owe to each other'. It should be said, finally, that there should of course be ways for noncitizens to become full members of a society. In other words, there ought to be pathways to complete political inclusion in a host country. But this is a different problem and not the subject of this study.

CONCLUSION

Issues of health justice are not confined to borders of nation-states. Traditionally issues of justice on a global scale have been conceived as concerning rights and duties of states, in analogy to domestic justice, where rights and duties of individual citizens are concerned. This leads to considerations of international justice. In recent years, a new way of devising theories of global justice has been developed. Cosmopolitanism sees individual people as the most basic unit of normative concern and accordingly interprets rights of people from a universal point of view.

As regards health justice more specifically, we have considered whether there is a human right to health and what that might encompass. The right was formulated as a right to have one's health-care needs met. However, what exactly that means in terms of health-care resources depends on many factors. Needs can be met in many different ways, and it is inadequate to assume that theories of justice alone can determine the content of an adequate package of health provision.

We have also scrutinised the normative significance of global health inequalities. Extreme inequalities in (proxies for) health of different populations may indicate injustices but as such do not directly imply unjust circumstances. The injustices that might be indicated are themselves not only to do with access to health care; they point at a variety of social determinants of health. In other words, health justice needs to be considered within a broader perspective of social justice.

Finally, we have reflected on the less-established issues regarding health justice for noncitizens. The fact that noncompatriots reside within host countries throws up additional normative concerns of 'domestic global justice'. We have mainly discussed moral concerns regarding possible discrimination of noncitizens and of equal access. I have argued that although everyone is owed access to publicly funded health-care institutions, it can be justifiable to prevent noncompatriots from accessing the same level of care that is provided compatriots. My argument is based on a distinction between issues of justice—which account for a minimal level of provision—and further political considerations, based on solidarity between compatriots. Altogether, my argument in this chapter can be seen in connection to my general support of a sufficientarian outlook.

Chapter Six

Curtailing Health Promotion

In a previous chapter I have stressed that the level of scarcity of health-care resources is at least partly driven by its demand, not merely by the limited supply. The economic notion of demand used here stands for entitlements to the use of health-care institutions. Such a perspective makes it abundantly clear that the quantitative level of scarcity of publicly funded health-care resources is driven by normative considerations, not just factual limitations. As we have also seen before, theories of health justice and real-life political decision making as well usually restrict the use of resources by way of rationing. Here restriction is a second step after acknowledging initially justified claims to a maximal amount and a factual assessment that not all of these claims can be fulfilled. In other words, the demand side is only restricted on the basis of limited resources. If there were more resources available, these would be used to address maximalist claims. Hence, claims themselves are not sufficiently assessed from a normative point of view.

In this chapter we will see that there are numerous processes that drive the expansion of demand. First, there is the possibility of conceptual expansion. Here, more and more health conditions are categorised under the umbrella term of disease. This process can be called *pathologisation*. Second, health-care measures can be expanded to address harms and disadvantages of people that were treated by other means. This is *medicalisation*. Third, the value of health can be expanded, both in its quantitative and qualitative aspects. Accordingly, health can be deemed of inflated value—this is the quantitative aspect—and it might be seen as a moral value—a kind of value health was not considered to have in the past. Call this *healthisation*.

The backdrop of the mentioned processes is a prevalent perception within many societies regarding the nature and function of health care and the value of health. In philosophy of medicine there is a related debate on the goals of medicine that we will also study in this chapter. Obviously societies and individual people might not be aware of their presumptions regarding the value of health or the goals of health-care institutions. The analysis pursued in this chapter is mainly intended to theoretically model different real-life developments. Hopefully it can make a contribution to enhancing our understanding of common assumptions in relevant public debates. Philosophical analysis should thereby lead to improved political deliberation. The chapter also criticises certain assumptions and developments in many modern societies. Overall, my argument aims at curtailing health promotion to a reasonable level of intensity.

PATHOLOGISATION

The very fact that the presence of disease is usually regarded as a sufficient criterion for granting a justified claim to use publicly funded health-care resources makes the concept of disease a likely target for expansion. There are numerous powerful groups that have an interest in such conceptual expansion: medical personnel, the pharmaceutical industry and patients themselves. Since there are both significant confusion and disagreement about the definition of disease as well, it is difficult to keep pertinent expansive interests at bay.

Pathologisation does not need to be a bad thing. It can help affected people overcome stigmatisation and sometimes even moral contempt by others. Obviously it can also help those patients to receive desperately needed support by public funds. There are numerous historical examples of such beneficial pathologisation—most importantly in the case of psychopathology. It should be stressed, however, that the beneficial aspects are mainly to do with the benefits of the social role of a patient. In the context of this study it is of course access to health-care resources that needs to be mentioned. There are numerous other problems that come with labelling something a disease. Most importantly, because so many people identify disease with an impairment of well-being—an identification that I have challenged in an earlier chapter—there are possible misperceptions of the quality of life of people with chronic disease or disabilities. Still, that fact alone would not constitute sufficient grounds for rejecting disease classification where it is fitting. Wrong perceptions can be tackled by other means than turning concepts into political battlegrounds.

Altogether, acknowledging a condition as a disease can have both positive and negative effects. From the point of view defended in this study, decisions whether a condition constitutes a case of disease need to be based on a theory of disease. First and foremost, a scientific foundation for such normatively relevant decisions should be sought. Still, people might be forgiven for mainly considering the balance of benefits and disadvantages of disease labels. This was the approach taken by the *British Medical Journal* when in 2002 it ran a vote on its website. The purpose was to identify conditions that were regarded as 'nondiseases'. A list of roughly two hundred potential nondiseases was assembled and then put to vote to the readers of the journal. Strictly speaking, the ballot did not ask voters to identify conditions they did not regard as diseases but to recognise instances of *nondisease*, referring to 'a human process or problem that some have defined as a medical condition but where people may have better outcomes if the problem or process was not defined in that way'[1]. It is therefore conceivable that voters were of the opinion that people who are affected by a condition are actually better off if it is not called a disease. This is compatible with the belief that the condition in question is indeed a disease; it is also compatible with being neutral about this issue. In brief, the exercise was not simply concerned with conceptual intuitions.

The BMJ's vote can teach us something interesting about the concept of disease. Going back to the example discussed in the first chapter of this book, imagine that a top biological journal would, in a similar way, run a vote about which organisms their readers considered nonmammals. They might add a specification that by *nonmammal* they mean 'an organism that some have defined as a mammal but where it may have better outcomes if it were not defined in that way'. I suspect it is a fair guess that most readers would find this exercise ludicrous. But why is the BMJ's ballot not absurd? Probably because the concept of disease has no sharp boundaries. There is not even an agreed standard definition of disease in medicine, and hence quarrels are not only possible about which conditions actually can be termed diseases but also about what *disease* means in the first place. Potentially any human condition and problem might belong to the extension of the concept of disease. Such a state of affairs allows pathologisation.

Medicine does not speak with one voice, and there are many different theories of disease. It is therefore impossible to merely refer to medical parlance if we want to find out whether a specific condition is a disease. A sensible way to deal with the mentioned pluralism of disease theories is to find out whether any theory suffers from logical flaws and can therefore be rejected. After weeding out flawed theories, there may still be a couple of plausible approaches left, and a further criterion to choose might be which theory best serves specific purposes. As mentioned in the first chapter, a pertinent social interest in connection with the concept of disease is its potential gatekeeping function. Usually we believe that diseases ought to be treated by publicly funded resources but not healthy conditions. Indeed, many real societies combine acknowledgement of disease with a prima facie claim to the use of publicly funded health-care resources. To prevent unnecessary costs for welfare-state institutions, it would be wise to endorse a theory of disease that prevents pathologisation of normal health conditions by offering clear-cut conceptual criteria.

To be sure, it does not seem right to choose theories on the basis of external interests. The best theory ought to be chosen on grounds of its scientific merits—that is, because it provides the most convincing explanation of the relevant phenomena. If the best available theory of disease maintains that a specific condition is a disease, then so be it. However, there are different reasonable ways to explain and define the phenomena. Hence, societies cannot merely leave to the best scientific evidence and theoretical worth the decision as to which health conditions should be acknowledged as disease and accordingly as implying claims for treatment. Curtailing pathologisation requires political decisions as well.

MEDICALISATION

Medicalisation is the most frequently used term when discussing the expansion of medicine into new territory. According to my suggestion, the notion is used to cover the expansion of the practice of health care. A common example is the treatment of disruptive behaviour of children by prescribing drugs. Because such use of medication is usually connected to having a diagnosis, medicalisation and pathologisation tend to be connected phenomena. After all, a disease label—in our example, it is attention deficit hyperactive disorder—might be needed to apply medical treatment. Still, there are examples of medicalisation that do not go along with pathologisation. Certain public-health measures, such as fluoridation of water and treatment of malnutrition, could be seen as examples of expanding a medical perspective to social issues that used to be dealt with by nonmedical means. Many risk factors for disease that are not themselves diseases—for instance, high blood pressure—are these days considered worthy of immediate medical attention. Finally, medical practices have been used to enhance athlete performances, which can also be understood as an expansion into the territory of the nonpathological.

Like pathologisation, medicalisation is not necessarily bad. Diseases ought to be treated by the medical profession, and people who suffer from diseases should have access to health-care resources. For instance, medicalising clinical depression helped patients win necessary treatment. As we have seen before, the actual status of some conditions—whether they are really types of diseases—is not always firmly determined. In such cases, it might be better to enable medical treatment, to give it the benefit of the doubt, as it were. There might also be situations where medical means are especially effective or even the only available options. For example, in emergencies quick fixes like ready-to-use foods might be advisable for the time being so that lives can be saved, although most people would probably prefer to see malnutrition eradicated by a more long-term political strategy.

On the other hand, if social ills are treated by medical means, possible social solutions might be forgotten or deemed inadequate. Important examples in this respect are to do with disadvantages—real or perceived—that come along with disability and medical impairment. People with disabilities rightly maintain that the disadvantages they encounter are often related to poor consideration in planning environments, not their physical or mental conditions. To attempt to 'fix' the person by medical means instead of rearranging the environment is often a wrong and possibly insulting strategy—although it is also important to acknowledge that some people with disabilities indeed want medical 'fixes'. Where medical means become monopolised, we can identify one of the downsides of medicalisation.

The causal interconnectedness of social conditions and health statuses makes it very difficult to avoid medicalisation. The latter is, as it were, the flip side of acknowledging the social determinants of health. For instance, we know that lack of access to recreational space and constant noise might lead to certain diseases or a deterioration of health in terms of a higher risk to fall ill. Given these connections, we might see certain environments themselves as pathological. The same applies to lifestyles as well. Indeed, we can see the development of certain health-care strategies to address social conditions in many modern societies—say, by incentivising physical exercise or by supplying nicotine replacement therapy for smokers. Again, I do not want to claim that these strategies are wrong, but they follow a different normative rationale than traditional medical treatment of disease.

Similarly, from a perspective of social-justice theory we are often interested in how to level the playing field between citizens who compete for certain benefits, such as jobs, or, more generally, for a good human life. Disadvantages do not only come in the form of disease, but many disadvantages can be alleviated by medical means, used as enhancements. From the point of view of egalitarian justice there seems to be a straightforward normative rationale for allowing public funds to be spent on medical enhancements. Hence this is another likely cause of medicalisation.

The main problem with medicalisation in the context of this study is the fact that it adds to health-care expense. These additional costs would need to be justified, since they do not follow the same normative rationale as treatment of pathological conditions. Admittedly, the highlighted normative difference and the associated criticism of using medical means outside the area of straightforward disease itself relies on certain assumptions about the goals of medicine. We will return to these considerations in a later section of this chapter.

HEALTHISATION

To be in good health is good for the person in this condition. That is why health is often discussed in relation to well-being and advantage. Considered in this way, health is what is usually called a *prudential value*. It is prudent to pursue health or to deem it valuable. How valuable health is for a person seems to be based on personal ideas as to what a good life consists of. Some people like to be fit and healthy and might invest a lot of effort and time in achieving this goal. Others might be less interested, perhaps because they balance the effort against other valuable pursuits. Healthisation is a process that inflates health as a personal value. It might result in a situation where people are criticised or deemed irrational if they attach a relatively lower value to health.

Healthisation can also result in moralising health. We have already seen a potential avenue for holding people responsible for their health condition. Given that treatment of ill health requires resources, to be inconsiderate of one's own health might be deemed a form of indirect harm to others, because it leads to an increase in the consumption of health-care resources. When individual health becomes an object of individual responsibility, it can easily be moralised.

Finally, health can also be interpreted as a public asset. In a global economy, where domestic economies compete for international investments, the relative level of the workforce's health is of vital collective importance. Here health promotion may become a governmental duty. It is important to see that this duty may go way beyond the duty to enable citizens to live a healthy life, which we have discussed before in relation to an individual right to health. In competitive scenarios, to reach a basic threshold of enablement is not enough. Relative considerations regarding the improvement of the citizenry's collective health will be on the political agenda. Accordingly, health will again be moralised, in a social sense, which is another aspect of healthisation.

It should be acknowledged that *healthisation* is a term that has hardly been used in the scholarly literature. Peter Conrad, who mainly focuses on medicalisation in his work, used a very similar notion, writing, 'With medicalization, medical definitions and treatments are offered for previous social problems or natural events; with healthicization, behavioral and social definitions are advanced for previously biomedically defined events (e.g., heart disease). . . . One turns the moral into the medical, the other turns health into the moral'[2]. According to Conrad, the main point of connection between healthisation and medicalisation is the conflation of two separate spheres that have different sets of norms: the medical and the social sphere. Relatedly, both processes lead to confusion over the best or most adequate agency to deal with respective problems.

Healthisation needs to be assessed against the backdrop of specific circumstances within different societies. Since these vary, it is difficult to generally comment on it. In many Western societies, medicine and, more generally, health-related institutions offer services to customers who want to improve their health. These services are usually paid for by individual customers and are offered in addition to the health service to patients that is paid for by public funds. For example, people might want to take yoga classes or get their teeth straightened. Since these days we know more about the social determinants of health, additional services for health promotion can be thought of: for instance, training to improve coping with work-related stress or time management.

It might seem strange to talk about yoga classes or courses for time management in relation to health. After all, these are probably mainly considered by customers to improve their personal well-being. However, one effect of the perspective of public health is indeed to acknowledge the ubiquitous nature of the possibilities of health promotion. As we have seen, medicine is only one area of the numerous determinants of health. Accordingly, healthisation can be seen at work in areas not usually considered.

Healthisation, according to the perspective we have pursued in this chapter, leads to an interpretation of organismic conditions in terms of social standing. Imperfect health is considered to be a disadvantage and accordingly to be a potential moral scandal. Undeserved health-related disadvantages are then assumed to be unfair and to require political efforts to level the playing field. Deserved disadvantages, however, are regarded as failures of individual responsibility. We have seen in the second chapter that positive health is an unlimited ideal. In consequence, every health-related disadvantage potentially manifests an individual moral failure or a social injustice when seen from this perspective. Since almost every social aspect can be a social determinant of health, health-related disadvantages are everywhere. Altogether, healthisation turns health conditions into moral conditions. Health improvements over and above the absence of disease are turned into a prescription—in both senses of the word.

To be fair, even if we avoid healthisation, specific social conditions and lifestyles can be, and often are, moralised, in that people are held responsible for, say, being poor. Hence healthisation does not seem to be the only, and perhaps not the most, problematic mechanism as regards moralisation. My point here is, however, that reframing health problems as moral problems might lead to faulty normative assessments, not that alternative processes are without their own problems.

Again, healthisation does not have to be a bad thing altogether. Indeed, it might be regarded beneficial to the pursuit of a just society, because social ills can be linked to health, which comes with its own normative significance. High levels of unemployment, for example, do not seem to morally engage many people these days. Redescribing unemployment as health risk can open up new avenues of moral engagement. However, the constant confusion of health and social norms seems to me to undermine reasonable political deliberation. First, social conditions that go along with certain statistical health risks, such as unemployment or low social status, are morally scandalised via their health impact and not via their direct impact on individual people, what seems to be more adequate—for instance, the harm of lacking meaningful occupation itself. Second, the value of health is mainly considered in competitive terms. In consequence, every physical or mental condition of human beings poses a potentially bad or unjust state, because it might be worse than other possible conditions. Such a constant overassessment and moralisation of health conditions can lead to further developments that I personally find worrisome as well. Put briefly, turning health into an asset easily leads to health care as a service for the worried well, who want to remain in an advantageous position. Eventually, it will undermine solidarity within societies and globally, because ill health is then mainly considered a product of moral fault, either of the individual or of the government. Health promotion is then not seen as a joint effort anymore.

GOALS OF MEDICINE

Some philosophers of medicine have criticised the expansion of medicine into new territories by arguing that medicine has particular intrinsic goals that restrict the proper use of medical means to the pursuit of these goals. According to such a view, the goals of medicine, such as treatment of disease and relief of suffering, are intrinsic goals insofar as they are implied by the practice itself. This is partly a traditional argumentation, going back as far as ancient philosophical ideas about actions and practices. Every action seems to aim at a goal; otherwise we would perhaps not even call it an action. Practices are iterated actions and also seem goal-oriented. They have, in philosophical terms, a telos, or a telic structure. For the argument about the goals of medicine, this general idea is important, as it paves the ground for assuming particular goals of the practice of medicine. It is more difficult, though, to establish these goals as intrinsic to the practice of medicine itself. Such reasoning seems to rely on an assumption of a particular nature or essence of medicine.

A prominent philosopher of medicine, who has argued the case for intrinsic goals of medicine, is Edmund Pellegrino. Alternatively, a task force at the Hastings Center—a leading bioethics academic institution—determined such goals of medicine in a process of identifying an international consensus. Although there might not be huge differences in terms of the mentioned goals of medicine between a teleological and a consensual approach, there are notable methodological differences. A consensual approach allows for the goals of medicine to change historically and socially, whereas a teleological approach aims at a universal and nonrelative determination of the proper goals of medicine. If the latter account would be convincing, we would have found a philosophical basis for rejecting expansions of medicine.

Discussion of the goals of medicine relies on a particular conception of medicine. But it is not quite clear what medicine encompasses or how to define the nature of medicine. It is often stated that medicine is both a science and an art. In other words, medicine has a theoretical part, which has to do mostly with gaining knowledge about the functions and dysfunctions of the organism. Medicine understood as an art is the application of such knowledge in specific contexts, such as diagnosis, treatment or prognosis. So the extension of the concept of medicine seems to be fairly broad, as many scientific endeavours and also quite a few practices seem to be aspects of medicine. In addition, there are other terms that are occasionally used synonymously with the concept of medicine—most importantly, *health care*. Health care includes practices such as nursing or rehabilitation. Finally, as we have discussed, there is the discipline of public health, which includes practices that aim at the health of the population. It uses the science of epidemiology and different practical means, such as information or health education, policies or the intentional shaping of the circumstances of people's choices. As we have seen throughout this study, there are indeed many practices that aim at health and the prevention of disease, including medicine, health care and public health. Even if some of these practices are not to be counted as medicine proper, it seems obvious that the goals of aiming at health and preventing disease are not specific to medicine. Hence, there is already a problem for determining the concept of medicine by reference to its alleged goals. *Medicine* does not have clear-cut boundaries, and it is impossible to conceptually separate medicine from other practices by referring to its alleged goals, because these goals are shared with several other disciplines. Since the nature of medicine is underdetermined, it cannot simply be assumed that medicine is a specific discipline or practice with clear-cut goals.

Another way to determine the goals of medicine is by interpreting it as a practice, which is structured by aiming in a certain direction. As mentioned, this is a traditional idea that goes back at least to ancient philosophy. Here the aims of practices also specify certain excellences or virtues. In a teleological approach, the telos—or end—of a practice determines the good it aims at. Virtues are accordingly the excellent ways to perform such practices. When discussing the goals of medicine, such an account requires some idea of the specific goods that medicine aims at. An obvious goal of medicine is health.

A well-known defender of such a teleological account of the goals of medicine is Edmund Pellegrino. He maintains, 'we must assert the obvious:

medicine exists because humans become sick. It is an activity conceived to attain the overall end of coping with the individual and social experience of disordered health. Its end is to heal, help, care and cure, to prevent illness, and cultivate health'[3].

It should be noted that Pellegrino allows for some level of change in using medicine for specific social purposes. Yet these purposes always need to be linked to the inherent ends of medicine. Hence there is no scope for taking medicine outside its proper remit, which is intrinsically set. The ends of medicine are determined by the practice of medicine, and these ends are essentially focused on sick patients.

Similarly, Leon Kass also maintains that there are proper goals of medicine. These set the norm for proper use of medical means. 'I am rather inclined to the old-fashioned view that health—or if you prefer, the healthy human being—is the end of the physician's art. That health is a goal of medicine few would deny. The trouble is, so I am told, that health is not the only possible and reasonable goal of medicine, since there are other prizes for which medical technique can be put in harness. Yet I regard these other goals—even where I accept their goodness as goals—as false goals for medicine, and their pursuit as perversions of the art'[4].

It does not seem likely that Pellegrino and Kass can make good their claim regarding proper goals of medicine. It is not even clear how exactly to draw the boundaries of the practice called medicine. In addition, one might wonder in what way the specific goals of medicine and the assumption of a teleological structure of the practice can be philosophically justified, especially given historical variations. It does not seem easy, and perhaps is impossible, to circumvent the normative debate about the proper use of medical means by a philosophical account of the proper goals of medicine.

A less metaphysically charged approach is put forward by a group of scholars at the Hastings Center discussing the goals of medicine. Their idea was to use philosophical argument and empirical evidence to assemble a list of plausible goals of medicine without assuming that it collects the only proper items of such a list. The methodology of such an approach can be called consensual, as it aims at an international consensus regarding the goals of medicine. Such a consensus requires deliberation and exchange of philosophical argument.

The group drafted the following list of four core goals of medicine: (1) prevention of disease and injury and promotion and maintenance of health, (2) relief of pain and suffering caused by maladies, (3) care and cure of those with a malady and care of those who cannot be cured and (4) avoidance of premature death and the pursuit of a peaceful death[5].

These goals are obviously not too different from the ones put forward by the defenders of the teleological approach. One pertinent difference, though, is implied by the final goal of avoidance of premature death. Depending on what precisely is meant by 'premature' death there might be room for justified medical interventions—for instance, the treatment of biologically normal deteriorations of fitness, which Pellegrino and Kass would not see as falling within the remit of medicine proper. In other words, the goal of avoiding premature death might justify enhancements—as opposed to treatment of disease.

Methodologically, the Hastings Center group seems to allow for revisions of their list, should there be considerable changes in social value judgements. After all, they assert 'crucial points of contact between medical goals and social goals'[6]. Hence it is not quite clear how the setting of goals can establish an independently valid norm of the proper use of medicine when using the methodology of consensus. Even practices many of us today might regard as instances of medicalisation might change their status if the viewpoints within society change accordingly. To be sure, reasonable exchange would still be needed within such methodology, not just a majority vote or the like. But be that as it may, there would be no external standard of the proper use of medical means, set by particular goals. This is to be expected within a consensual approach. It necessarily involves an element of conventionalism.

Alternative lists of goals of medicine have been proposed in the relevant literature. These are fairly similar to the mentioned list, though they include additional aspects, such as tackling the social determinants of health and reassuring the 'worried well'. Still, such similarity suggests a widespread convergence in normative assessments of the point of medicine and its remit—at least within a certain shared cultural background and at a particular point in time. It seems adequate to expect an ongoing debate about the goals of medicine in philosophy of medicine. This is at least partly due to the continuing dispute regarding the moral limits of the use of medical means to treat undesired ailments and to enhance desired conditions.

The main target of the scholarly debate on the goals of medicine has been to establish normative conclusions about the moral limits of the use of medicine for individual or social purposes. It has been claimed by some that the proper goals of medicine exclude certain medical practices—for instance, enhancements of fitness, aesthetic goals, the use of medicine in hastening death or other contested desires. I have argued in this section, however, that it is neither methodologically nor substantively straightforward that such a conclusion can be reached via an exploration of the goals of medicine. The debate on such goals is philosophically significant in its own right, but it is doubtful that ethical issues can be solved on its basis. They need to be connected to considerations of social justice and political goals more widely.

CONCLUSION

In this chapter we have examined several processes that lead to an expansion of the demand of health care in real societies. We have distinguished pathologisation, medicalisation and healthisation. Mainly these processes are due to confusion regarding the boundaries of social ills as opposed to medical problems. Given the increasing knowledge about the social determinants of health, the mentioned processes are perhaps unavoidable. Yet they should be viewed with a certain amount of scepticism because they can lead to moral and political misjudgement.

A possible way to curtail health promotion into adequate channels would be to identify the correct goals of medicine. These would then set the target of health promotion more generally. However, theories that speculate about an alleged nature of medicine face severe theoretical difficulties. A more adequate methodology of determining goals of medicine indicate that curtailing health promotion is, after all, a political task that requires practical deliberation. Philosophical considerations can support such deliberation, but they cannot solve the issues for us.

Chapter Seven

A Sufficientarian Theory of Health Justice

In this chapter, I will defend a sufficientarian account of health justice. I mentioned in the third chapter that the basic idea of the theory is to provide enough health for all. This is an abstract goal that requires some elucidation. In order to say more about what 'enough health' means, we need to return to conceptual considerations regarding health and disease. We will also discuss why health is an important value for human beings and reasons for seeing its maintenance as a political task, which generates issues of social justice. Earlier chapters have laid the groundwork for our considerations in this chapter. We can now dig a little deeper and defend a particular viewpoint. Obviously readers might want to disagree with some of the claims made here. If everything has gone the way intended in writing this book, then they will also know the reasons why they disagree and how to argue for an alternative theory of health justice.

I will, first of all, strengthen the case for disentangling the concept of disease from evaluative connotations. In other words, I want to show that disease is not necessarily bad for the affected person. This is important to acknowledge, because it allows us to make a case, second of all, in favour of a theory of health justice that sees the main normative concern of disease in its impact on a person's life and, more generally, her achievement of goals, not in the fact that it is causing comparative disadvantage. We have then built a foundation for a third step in the argument, which aims at establishing a noncomparative account of justice as the preferred perspective for issues of health justice. Such a perspective puts the notion of needs at centre stage. The chapter ends, fourth of all, with fleshing out in a little bit more detail what sufficientarianism about health justice means and how to make decisions about rationing.

It should perhaps be stressed, again, that a theory of disease serves important normative functions, although it is not itself solving issues of health justice. The concept of disease sets the boundaries for justified claims of justice; at least in its naturalist variant it can curtail processes that expand such claims. That is why a theory of disease is a relevant part of a theory of health justice.

IN WHAT SENSE IS IT BAD TO HAVE A DISABILITY?

As we have noticed in the first chapter of this book, many theories of disease identify a conceptual connection between disease and harm. According to this viewpoint, usually called *normativism*, ill health is a type of harm by definition. In this section I will implicitly argue against normativism, although my main concern is an evaluative problem seen from a naturalist point of view. I will refer to chronic forms of disease and impairments—summarised under the umbrella term *disability*—because they seem to be the most unlikely cases for making my argument good. If it can be shown that even long-term and incurable pathological conditions are not necessarily bad, then I have made my case for disentangling evaluation and explanation of pathological conditions as strongly as possible.

It is common to see disability as an instance of harm. For example, John Harris claims that disabilities are 'physical or mental conditions that constitute a harm to the individual, which a rational person would wish to be without'[1]. Tristram Engelhardt asserts that 'to see a phenomenon as . . . a disability is to see something wrong with it'[2]. The received view contends that to be disabled means to have suffered a kind of loss, to be disadvantaged in certain respects or to be in a deficient physical or mental condition. Many different terms can be utilised for these kinds of negative evaluations of disability, though generally they all follow the same pattern, asserting that disability is bad for the person who has it.

This received view regularly clashes with the viewpoint of people with disabilities. At least some of them claim that they are not harmed by their condition. For instance, Mark Zupan, a quadriplegic rugby player, maintains, 'My injury has led me to opportunities and experiences and friendships I would never have had before. And it has taught me about myself. In some ways, it's the best thing that ever happened to me'[3]. A psychiatric patient says, 'Gee, you know, they're telling me this is a disease. If it's a disease, this is the one I want to have. . . . I look at myself as privileged to have had the experiences I had, the experiences they call pathology'[4]. It is easy, on the basis of the received view, to read such statements as rationalisations of disastrous events, as attempts to find meaning in senseless harm. But I believe that the quotations put forward a truthful, indeed rational, point of view.

Some readers might, at this point, argue that the good things that might come with disability are inconclusive to assess disability. After all, people like Zupan might be even better off if they had enjoyed the same experiences without becoming quadriplegic. In philosophical terms, this would mean that, 'all things being equal' (ceteris paribus), Zupan is worse off. I will accept this argument. However, I will maintain that medical impairments do not need to be seen as intrinsically, or noncomparatively, harmful, even though they might be worse than other possible conditions. The distinction is important, because it highlights two different kinds of harm.

It should also be acknowledged that the normativist theory does not need to clash with the perspective of some people with disabilities. After all, Harris and other authors seem to be concerned with a conceptual question. They might simply accept that Zupan and other people who do not suffer in consequence do not have a disability. I doubt that normativists would actually make this argument, but for my argument this problem is immaterial.

Disability is due to both impairment—that is, intrinsic features of the affected organism—and the environment—that is, disabling circumstances, such as documents written in a complicated style of writing. Since these causes come in various degrees of combination, there can be some debate as to whether disability is a medical concept—because of the impairment of organismic functions—or a social concept—because of the environmental conditions. The debate over the nature of disability has continued for many years, resulting in the development of a medical versus a social model of disability.

It seems to me that the debate about models is really concerned with the problem of evaluation rather than with classification and labelling. The relevant question seems to be whether or not a disability is necessarily bad for the affected person, not whether or not we can call it a medical condition. It seems pretty obvious that Zupan, the quadriplegic rugby player, has a medical condition—he cannot walk—but this does not say much about the general value of walking or about the assessment of not being able to walk from Zupan's individual perspective. The latter is what the social model of disability focuses on: the impact of a medical condition on a person's life.

But can it really be reasonable to doubt that chronic disease or impairment is harmful? Disability as an experience in people's lives apparently needs to be evaluated negatively in each and every instance. A supporting argument for this standpoint stems from a debate in bioethics. It concerns the prohibition of causing impairment—for instance, to a foetus. It seems that if disability were not to be necessarily disvalued—if it were a 'mere difference'—it would be allowable to actively cause disability. But that would be imprudent, to say the least. Similarly, it would be perfectly reasonable to reject possible cures or scientific studies to find cures for disability, as we normally want to cure what we believe is bad for us. In contrast to this argument, I believe that people with disabilities can desire a cure for disability without agreeing that disability is necessarily bad for them. There is no incoherence involved in these two judgements, because there is a distinction between a comparative and a noncomparative perspective on disability. Disability can be comparatively worse than a contrasting condition, but it need not be bad for the affected person as judged by itself.

The well-being of humans can be affected in two different ways: Something that impacts their well-being can be harmful in itself, such as a life-threatening disease or the experience of pain. But harm can also be present when a person's situation is worsened—for instance, when a fire destroys her house. Here, whether something is harmful depends on a comparison with the situation a person was in before an event happened. It is important to realise that a comparative harm need not always be a case of noncomparative—that is, absolute—harm. When a person loses money in a gamble, she is worse off than before, but she is not necessarily harmed in an absolute way by the loss. The latter would likely be the case, though, if her financial means were to fall below a standard of sufficiency because of the loss.

Comparative harm is certainly something we deem negative and unwanted. We normally do not want to be worse off in any aspect of our lives. This is similar in terms of conditions of health, disease and disability. For instance, almost everyone will prefer not to be allergic to certain substances—say, garlic—and hence deem having a garlic allergy to be a comparative harm. But there can be pathological conditions that people are neutral about, such as being dyslexic in an environment where written communication is obsolete or being short-sighted in a community that secures access to glasses or contact lenses. The evaluative assessment of comparative harms depends not only on subjective evaluations but also on the circumstances a person lives in—that is, whether a particular disease or disability poses a real disadvantage. For some people, it would not be a sufficient compensation of the comparative harm of short-sightedness to wear glasses, for instance, because they cannot do the job they want to do anymore.

Regarding disability, I believe it is plausible to maintain that people normally prefer to be healthy and hence deem disability a case of comparative harm. The persons cited before even prefer the condition of ill health, but for my argument I do not need to support this stronger claim. I should think that even people with disabilities who claim that they are not in a harmed condition could agree with the notion of comparative harm involved in disability, because it is not the kind of harm they refer to. They do not worry about the comparative worth of a disability but about its absolute impact on their lives. But just as not everyone needs to see it as a harmful condition in absolute terms if she cannot eat garlic, not everyone needs to see a disability as harmful, absolutely speaking.

Comparative harm is due to comparing different states or conditions of organisms, in our case of human beings. There is an important issue as to what conditions might be used as contrast. I will not be able to say much about this, but surely it cannot be any conceivable condition. A human being is not comparatively harmed, for instance, by the fact that she cannot fly. The cases we deal with—having an organismic dysfunction in contrast to being medically normal—restrict the set of possible comparisons accordingly to typical or ordinary conditions of human beings.

It seems to me that a health condition is regarded as harmful in absolute terms when an affected person cannot identify with it, or, rather, cannot integrate it in her self-conception. To evaluate whether a condition is absolutely harmful, it will be assessed in its own right, not in comparison to another condition, such as being medically normal. To be noncomparatively harmful, a condition need not be consciously experienced as harmful—for instance, as painful—but it needs to be something the affected person cannot endorse or see as part of herself; it is something the person wants to be rid of. This allows for disparate judgements regarding the harmfulness of a specific condition. For example, a man can certainly prefer not to lose his hair but still insist that he does not think the condition of being bald is harmful to him in its own right. This is because being bald can be part of his identity, or, rather, because being bald might not be regarded as serious enough to be alien to him.

I readily admit that my description of the source of seeing something as noncomparatively harmful in terms of not being able to identify with it is rather vague. But the notion of identity is helpful, I believe, because disability almost by its nature is, or can become, a part of a person's identity. Disability is different from a passing disease. It is a condition a person was born with or will be in for a long time, maybe the rest of her life. This helps us explain the apparent paradox that most people would deem ill health to be absolutely harmful, though not everyone sees a disability—which can be described as a kind of chronic disease—as harmful in this way. A chronic condition can become a part of a person's identity, whereas this seems more difficult with passing diseases. It also provides a plausible explanation as to why people with congenital disabilities more regularly deny the absolute harmfulness of the disability than people with acquired disabilities. This is because for them the medical impairment has always been a part of their identity. For others, disability needs to become a part of their identity before they can make the same claim. Well-being is closely related to one's identity, and it is therefore to be expected that once a disability has gradually become 'internalised', its noncomparative harmfulness also gradually decreases.

Altogether we can say that disability might always be a comparative harm. It might always be worse to be disabled than to be healthy. Admittedly, even that might be too strong, as some people might reasonably prefer to be disabled. However, as I have said above, the stronger claim is not required for my argument, since I want to argue that disability is not necessarily an absolute harm. What I have agreed with as regards comparative harm accounts for the common description of disability as making people worse off, being a detriment or posing a disadvantage. These are all comparative notions. The comparative aspects of disabilities can often be mitigated such that they do not necessarily have permanent (comparative) harmful effects. The most discussed example in this respect is the compensating effect of sign language for deaf people. Although we can agree that disability might be considered harmful in comparative terms, what is more important is whether it necessarily is a harm in noncomparative terms. I have argued that this is not the case, because disability can become, or often is, part of a person's identity. This means that it is an individual matter whether disability is bad for the person affected; hence, the received view, which can be read to maintain that medical impairment is always a harmed condition, is false.

Someone might object that the difference between a comparative and noncomparative evaluation is less important than I have claimed, indeed, that we can always turn the absolute perspective into a comparative one if we include alternative, hypothetical situations. The person who had an accident or who was born blind could have had another life, or she might be cured in a conceivable world. We simply need imagination to do this kind of comparison. I believe this is correct, and I have not claimed that we cannot perform this kind of change of perspective. I merely defended the argument that often people do in fact take a noncomparative evaluative stance towards aspects of their lives and that this might differ from a comparative one because the particular aspect is regarded as an integral element of who they are. To take a comparative perspective regarding this particular aspect is certainly still possible, and it can indeed lead to a form of ambivalence in the evaluation that we often find in people with disabilities. My main aim in this section was to reject arguments that tend to focus only on comparative aspects and accordingly claim that ill health is necessarily bad for the affected person.

This result is important because we can now clearly distinguish—for the purposes of health justice—two different goals of health care: to alleviate absolute harm and to alleviate comparative harm. The first aims at individual well-being, broadly conceived—specifically, at making the affected person 'whole' again in terms of a unified identity. The second goal aims at compensating for disadvantage that comes with ill health. The argument so far also allows us to appreciate that disease and disability do not necessarily involve harm in all relevant respects and that alleviating harm does not always require medical treatment.

DISABILITY AS DISADVANTAGE

Disability is of course an important example of the kind of disadvantage that is of interest to theorists of social justice. It is a condition that is in almost all cases a matter of unchosen bad luck; and it makes disabled people worse off than others. Since for egalitarians 'it is unjust for one to be worse off than others through no fault of one's own'[5], disability seems to be a clear-cut case of raising concerns of justice. However, as argued in the previous section, it is not straightforward whether, and, if so, in what respect, disability makes people worse off than others. I now want to scrutinise what it means to interpret disability as disadvantageous.

I want to argue that there is an important distinction between a comparative and a noncomparative interpretation of disadvantage, similar to the distinction between comparative and absolute harm. For the sake of clarity, I will use the term *relative disadvantage* for the former and *hurdle* for the latter interpretation. It might well be that disability prevents a person from achieving a goal without support or compensation. Yet if relevant agencies try to help that person to achieve the goal, they are focusing on such hurdles and how to overcome them. They usually do not compare the situation of a person with a disability to any other person's likelihood of achieving the same goal. Accordingly, disability does not have to be interpreted as a relative disadvantage. To identify a relative disadvantage requires interpersonal comparisons, but depending on the goals we aim at, what is needed on grounds of justice by each person is not determined by such comparisons. Relative disadvantage is not the main problem of justice. The example of disability can indeed establish why a comparative perspective may sometimes undermine the very purposes of justice and occasionally be derogative to people with disabilities.

Anita Silvers refers to the example of the deaf child Amy Rowley, who was not provided with a sign language interpreter in her school, which otherwise generally catered to children with disabilities. Although Amy was a prolific lip-reader and received further support by a hearing aid, speech therapists and special tutors, she was only able to understand about half of the conversations in the classroom. While Amy performed better than the average students, it seems intuitive to say that she was relatively disadvantaged. Indeed Silvers explicitly states, 'With access to only half the instruction and information her peers received in class, she lacked the same opportunity as hearing children to develop her intellectual talents'[6]. It is important to note that Silvers specifies in what respect Amy was disadvantaged; it was not simply a matter of being deaf that made Amy worse off but the lack of sufficient provision to enable her to develop her intellectual talents. Silvers does not stress the fact that Amy suffered a relative disadvantage—she actually performed better than average—but that her talents apparently would have allowed for enhancing her skills and knowledge even more had she not been held back by her insufficiently compensated deafness. Hence Silvers is pointing out a hurdle in relation to a goal—in this case the purpose of developing one's intellectual talents.

Yet when Amy's parents sued the school for failing to provide a sign language interpreter, their charge was rejected by the Supreme Court on the grounds that 'the statutory mandate of a "free appropriate public education" had been satisfied by allowing Amy to be in class and to learn'[7]. Hence, the Supreme Court did not disagree that Amy encountered a disadvantage in developing her talents, but it disagreed about the purpose of schooling for disabled people. On the basis of this interpretation of the goal, Amy was not seen to be hindered by a hurdle: 'The opinion declared that . . . for handicapped children educated alongside their nondisabled peers, educational benefit was demonstrated by a plan reasonably calculated "to open the door of public education to handicapped children by means of specialized educational services but not to guarantee any particular substantive level of education once inside"'[8].

I do not intend to challenge the substance of the Supreme Court's verdict itself, yet it shows something important: The general point this ruling establishes is that hurdles need to be specified in relation to particular goals. We need to discuss the means people need in order to achieve a goal when thinking about whether they face a hurdle. According to the Supreme Court's ruling, Amy was not facing a hurdle in pursuing the stated goal of education for disabled children—namely, to enable access to public education. Neither a particular substantive level of education nor a comparatively similar competitive capacity like her nondisabled peers was seen as the goal. We can of course quarrel with this interpretation of the goal of education, but my point is that it will be the first question of justice in education—namely, what we should aim at when educating children. The same idea applies to health justice. The most basic question we need to answer before we discuss hurdles that ought to be overcome by the provision of health care is what the aims of heath-care institutions are.

By acknowledging the fact that disadvantages need to be specified in relation to goals, we can now see that the concepts of disadvantage or being disadvantaged can be used comparatively or noncomparatively. In a comparative way we can speak of disadvantage when we compare two states, qualities, and so forth and conclude that someone is less likely than others to reach a given goal. It would be a comparative disadvantage, for example, to have a cold when running a marathon. Here we look at the likelihood that a goal will be reached, which is, for instance, less likely when someone is in a condition of impaired health in comparison to normal health.

Disadvantage can also be transformed into a noncomparative concept, whereby necessary means for pursuing a goal are determined. If these are not available, a person suffers from a disadvantage that I have called a 'hurdle'. In Amy's case, the Supreme Court held that Amy was not hindered in her pursuit of public education; it was claimed that this 'door was open' to her so that in fact the necessary means for achieving the stated goal were accessible to her. A disadvantage in the noncomparative sense is understood as something that significantly undercuts a person's capacity of achieving a goal, which is not the same as worsening the likelihood compared to other person's chances. In this sense, it would not be a hurdle to have a cold while running a marathon, because one could still finish the marathon, and even win; the runner has all the necessary means of achieving the specified goal. Noncomparative disadvantage, therefore, occurs whenever someone falls below a standard of what is seen to be the necessary requirements for reaching that goal. A cold does not prevent someone from finishing a marathon, and neither does it even prevent someone from coming in first place, if that is the goal.

In this section I offered two interpretations of disadvantage. In the noncomparative sense—that is, in the sense of being confronted with a significant obstacle to pursue a goal—not every disability has to be a hurdle. In a comparative sense, disability can be understood more generally as a disadvantage if we claim that disabilities always worsen affected people's chances of pursuing goals whenever their health states are compared to bodily or mental constitutions that are considered healthy. More importantly, I have tried to establish that the specific disadvantages, if any, of disability need to be specified in relation to goals. This claim can be generalised: disadvantages are present when persons have either worse chances than other people for reaching a goal (comparative disadvantage) or when they lack necessary means to reaching a goal (noncomparative disadvantage).

NONCOMPARATIVE EQUALITY OF OPPORTUNITY

Previously I mentioned the normative usage of the concept of disadvantage, which we find in many egalitarian theories. According to this point of view, a disadvantage is something that should be removed or that deserves compensation. Here we are moving more directly into the realm of the debate on social justice and especially the debate on equality of opportunity as a goal of justice.

Now, perhaps not surprisingly, the distinction between comparative and noncomparative can also be applied to opportunities; in fact, we have used such a distinction implicitly before. The notion of opportunity is often used to refer to a chance someone has to do something, like buying a house or getting a job. Obviously an opportunity in this sense does not imply that the person actually gets what she has the chance to get. There might be reasons for her to forgo, there might be competitors who are better suited or, more interesting for our discussion, there might be disadvantages that inhibit or impair her ability to compete. The ideal of equal opportunity is invoked in this context of competition. According to a common understanding, opportunities are equal when people can compete on fair terms; this implies as a necessary condition that there are no (undeserved) advantages or disadvantages. It is important to note that in competitive scenarios each competitor's opportunity, or chance, to succeed is dependent on the other competitors' situation and performance. How likely it is that someone wins a prize, for example, depends partly on the presence, motivation, skill, endowment and fitness of other participants. Since individual competitive opportunity is only assessable in contrast to other people, this notion of opportunity is comparative.

But the notion of opportunity can also be assessed in a noncomparative way. Opportunities in this sense are closer to effective freedoms or capabilities. For instance, people might have the opportunity to cycle to work or to read books. Whether and to what degree a person's opportunities in this sense are diminished by certain conditions, such as ill health, is not dependent on other people's skills, fitness or endowments. Person A's opportunities are, then, not dependent on person B's situation but only on A's own endowments, skills, bodily and psychological fitness, environment, and so on.

Some egalitarians waver between a comparative and a noncomparative interpretation of opportunity and justice. For instance, when Norman Daniels discusses the idea of a 'normal opportunity range' that every person should be able to achieve (as far as possible), he might be read as to opt either for an absolute, noncomparative claim of justice of having certain abilities or effective freedom—normal opportunities in the sense of a fixed range of abilities—or for the comparative aspect of preventing disadvantages—to prevent persons from having fewer opportunities or options than others. In Daniels's case, much depends on how we translate the notion of normality in 'normal opportunity range': Either as a noncomparative standard that is, for instance, based on an objective notion of health or as a comparative standard that is determined by the opportunities that other people have. Similarly, Jonathan Wolff and Avner de-Shalit refer to a 'lack of genuine opportunity for secure functioning'[9] when discussing disadvantage. The expression sounds noncomparative, because what secure functioning requires apparently is not dependent on the comparative standing of persons.

Just as for the concept of disadvantage, then, there are two ways to interpret the discourse on equal opportunities. For better terminological clarification of the ideal's two interpretations, we can divide equality of opportunity into comparative and noncomparative equality of opportunity, similar to a distinction between substantive and formal equality of opportunity, which is frequently found in the philosophical debate. Comparative equality of opportunity occurs if a person has roughly the same chance of reaching a goal as others do. Noncomparative equality of opportunity occurs if a real possibility of reaching a goal exists for everyone.

According to a noncomparative interpretation of justice, hurdles exist in one of two ways:

1. It is an undeserved obstacle that gets in a person's way when she pursues a goal and that should have been removed according to the already established standards. This is a case of *present injustice*.
2. Or it is a constraint on a person's capacity to pursue a goal that is not yet acknowledged as a hurdle, in which case the really relevant requirements for actually reaching that goal are not fulfilled. This is a case of *anticipated injustice*.

These two kinds of cases can lead to two different demands of noncomparative justice:

1. The first form concerns hurdles encountered when aiming at a standard—for instance, when people have to constantly live in a noisy environment. It wouldn't really be possible to achieve the goal of recreation in such conditions.
2. A second way to demand noncomparative justice attacks the standard itself, opting for another—for instance, when medical treatment is found inadequate for the specific needs of children. It is then claimed that the offered means to reach the goal of health should be reformed.

Because equal opportunity should serve as a normative criterion for social justice, it seems that the comparative interpretation as such does not offer much help in addressing issues of justice—for it does not generate a normative content but, rather, operates mostly on statistical likelihoods. These likelihoods, however, cannot be more than a potential symptom of a noncomparative hurdle that people face in pursuing a goal. Hence, normatively speaking, the noncomparative perspective has priority. After all, a person's prospects require a normative evaluation in order to figure out whether a relatively small chance of reaching a goal actually raises a problem of justice in the first place. Egalitarians, in virtue of their focus on comparative standing of persons, instead potentially see every difference in individual likelihoods to achieve certain goals as unjust. In contrast, I believe we should not be primarily concerned with assessing relative disadvantages, although they might have indirect significance for identifying hurdles. We should focus, rather, on the question as to what standards should look like; these determine how and whether the requirements for reaching a goal have been fulfilled.

These requirements affect first and foremost the legal and material means to which everyone is entitled. At the same time, in order to be just, it will also have to be ensured that these requirements are provided in a way that allows success for all and does not arbitrarily exclude people. To allow success for all obviously does not guarantee success for all; hence we are still talking about opportunities here. If we focus on noncomparative standards that state the requirements for enablement, we are no longer concerned with equal opportunities but with making opportunities available for all.

The discussion regarding which standards actually enable everyone to achieve certain goals will never been concluded but is, rather, a part of an ongoing general discussion about social justice on the level of society. It follows from all of this that a disability, especially if it is not compensated, can constitute a hurdle, but this does not necessarily have to be the case, because we first need to specify the goal of a certain aspect of life. Furthermore, it follows that it is not helpful, for the purposes of justice, to understand disability generally as a comparative disadvantage, because injustice needs to be specified according to standards of necessary means to pursue goals—that is, in the form of noncomparative injustice.

COMBINING NATURALISM WITH SUFFICIENTARIANISM

In contrast to egalitarianism, sufficientarianism generates individual entitlements without taking comparative assets of other people into account. What we owe to each other is determined in terms of absolute standards because what a person needs is not influenced by the circumstances other people live in but by her situation. Absolute harm is, in contrast to comparative disadvantage, not determined by an interpersonal comparison.

Sufficientarianism is not concerned with whether or not persons are worse off than others but with helping those who are badly off. Disease is regarded as a foundation for a justified claim on health-care resources if and when it is harmful in absolute, not in comparative, terms to the person who is affected by it. As we have seen, not every disease, however, must involve this kind of absolute harm. Still, most diseases are harmful at least for some people and would therefore justify a claim for using publicly funded health-care resources. It is at this stage that a restricted theory of disease—naturalism—does its useful work—namely, preventing the expansion of the concept of disease on grounds of social or individual evaluations.

There are some problems for naturalism about disease as a basis of restrictions on health-care resources that I want to discuss and eventually reject. First, there seems to be a straightforward way to justify a claim to publicly funded health-care resources even if a specific treatment cannot be regarded as treatment of disease—namely, by interpreting some medical interventions as a form of of preventive treatment. It could be argued, for example, that if a specific condition were not treated, a clinical depression might likely develop in consequence. Of course, clinical depression then must be accepted as pathological on naturalist premises. Even an enhancement—for instance, cosmetic surgery—could be justified by the same rationale as an instance of a justified claim on publicly funded health-care resources. The restrictive function of the naturalist account would be undermined by this indirect justification of claims via preventive measures.

A second problem for the naturalist point of view is posed by cases where no organismic dysfunction can be proven and yet it is assumed that a person has a disease anyway—probably a disease yet unknown to medical science. This line of reasoning provides a possible foundation for the expansion of the concept of disease by inventing new kinds of dysfunctions—an alleged anticipation of their scientific discovery.

Third, one might object to a naturalist foundation of health-care justice that entitlements to medical resources are not only based on treatment and prevention of disease. The treatment of many unwanted and unpleasant conditions is publicly funded, although they are not instances of disease. For example, doctors perform abortions, and they treat conditions related to the normal and natural process of ageing, like postclimacteric osteoporosis, which is not a pathological condition according to naturalism.

I believe that these objections merely establish that the naturalist theory of disease needs to be supported by genuinely evaluative considerations in order to be useful for issues of health justice. The naturalist theory of disease is not suited for the task of directly restricting entitlements to medical services. To find a way to tackle the problem of the ever-increasing budgets for funding health-care resources in modern societies, we need a normative point of view. And it seems that the main shortcoming of the naturalist account is the very lack of such a perspective. Prima facie, every pathological condition—even very minor dysfunctions—seems to justify a claim to medical treatment. The combination of the value we usually attach to health and the naturalist definition of health as normal functional ability apparently leads to an approach that includes treatment of every pathological condition in the package of basic health-care supply.

But since naturalism does not include evaluations, it does also not provide a foundation for the direct justification of the treatment of every disease as individual entitlement. Naturalism does not include a premise that every disease needs to be regarded as an instance of harm. Naturalism does, by itself, restrict the relevant putative cases for claiming health-care resources, as only disease, not lack of perfect positive health, is normatively relevant. Within the realm of disease, an appropriate evaluative supplement needs to be added for restricting justified health-care demand.

I have already agreed that it is possible to assert that every impairment of functional ability causes a relative disadvantage—and hence a kind of comparative harm. But, again, only egalitarianism would regard every disadvantage as a potential injustice. Since I want to defend a combination of naturalism and sufficientarianism, the mentioned objection that it is not possible to restrict entitlements with the help of a naturalist theory of disease does not apply to my account. I submit that an account of health justice that combines the purpose of alleviating noncomparative harm with a scientific definition of potential medical harm in terms of organismic dysfunction can indeed limit entitlements to publicly funded health-care resources in a reasonable way. In brief, I believe a combination of naturalism about disease and sufficientarianism about justice will be well suited for modern welfare states.

SUFFICIENTARIAN HEALTH JUSTICE

The goal of health-care institutions can be described as providing the necessary means for everyone to lead healthy lives and to be able to make healthy choices, not to make people equally healthy or as healthy as possible. It is concerned with achieving an aim that can be described as 'enabling the playing field'. Admittedly this idea is still fairly abstract. In the end, I believe, it will have to be fleshed out by real societies in political processes.

Health provision is a political task. It is part of the remit of every welfare state. In order to understand the proper role of health care and public health it is therefore helpful to discuss it in the wider context of state action, particularly the purpose of a welfare state. More concretely, we might want to phrase the question, How much of a concern for the state is the health of the population? I understand this question not merely to pose problems of normative political theory alone; it needs to be answered in the context of the real worlds of welfare states. This commitment to a more realist political outlook can build on some of the methodological considerations we have discussed in the third chapter.

I will argue that a minimalist understanding of the general purpose of welfare states is to demand the inclusion of every citizen into society. The basic idea is that every citizen should be included as a member of a society; the aim is focused on the social status of citizens. Such an abstract description allows for various concrete provisions and diverging emphases on values that flesh out the idea of inclusion. Accordingly, there can be several variants of just welfare states. Also, whether people are able to deem themselves to be members of a particular society can require different provisions relative to the level of development. For instance, if the majority of people within a society have access to computers and modern media, it might be possible that citizens who cannot provide for access to these media by themselves are excluded from society in this respect. More pertinent to our discussion, in a society that lives for an average of eighty years it can be a sign of possible exclusion if some people die in their fifties due to their living conditions. Hence the exact location of thresholds of inclusion can be relative to the societal and historical context. Still, in each case there is a relevant noncomparative threshold set by the idea of inclusion—or, more accurately, the prevention of exclusion.

There exist important connections of this idea with the theory of relational egalitarianism. I have mentioned briefly in the third chapter that some aspects of relational egalitarianism are rather to be seen as nonegalitarian—and hence in close vicinity to sufficientarianism. Still, the type of sufficientarianism I endorse is different from relational egalitarianism in that the idea of inclusion is not fleshed out in terms of how individual citizens relate to others—though this is part of the idea—but whether everyone is enabled to live a decent life. In other words, inclusion is here understood to belong to a set of people who have access to certain goods, not as an interpersonal relation.

To focus on the idea of social inclusion in relation to the aims of the welfare state is not an unusual idea. In fact, it can be found in one of the most advanced and renowned theories of the origins of the welfare state: Thomas H. Marshall's *Citizenship and Social Class*[10]. Marshall distinguishes between social rights according to their historical development: first, civil or liberty rights, often called negative rights because they restrict the justified use of state and societal power; second, political rights, such as the right to vote and gain political power; third, social rights, which entitle citizens to accessing social goods, such as health care. According to Marshall, the expansion of rights can be interpreted as an increasing inclusion of citizens under the notion of citizenship. Accordingly, citizens become full members of society. The aim of welfare-state institutions is to safeguard citizens' rights by preventing exclusion. The level of such provision is constantly to be debated within society and cannot be set by a philosophical theory of justice. Welfare states are therefore sites of struggles between different conceptions of justice, where there is no one correct theory of justice. Still, theoretical considerations regarding a minimal threshold might be possible.

What might the abstract purpose of inclusion mean for health care, including public health? The answer to this question depends on the actual requirements of living a minimally healthy life, and, hence, at least partly on empirical findings. For instance, providing the necessary means will have educational aspects, such as informing citizens about threats to health and how they can improve health dispositions. More specifically, health education will involve information about nutrition, stress and unhealthy lifestyles—in general such education will aim at so-called health literacy. Providing the means for inclusion will also have circumstantial aspects, such as providing access to medical care, to recreational activity and protection from hazardous substances or epidemics. All of these measures aim at a sufficient level of enablement of a minimally healthy life, which allows citizens to feel as members of society, in contrast to improving individual and population health over and above such a threshold.

A fitting example of a sufficientarian public-health measure that stays within the limits of enough health is the public funding of school meals. A certain amount of food per day is a necessary requirement for human beings to live a healthy life. Another aspect of having school meals is the collective experience of pupils. To be excluded from school lunches for economic reasons not only very likely means the affected child will be less adequately nourished but also implies the child will not be part of a group sharing a valuable experience; and perhaps there are additional ill effects, such as the student's being stigmatised, which might have long-term consequences for psychological health as well. Now, obviously school meals could be provided in different ways: schools could leave it up to the students to pick from several food options, or perhaps the students would be given no choice in the menu because of a worry that some kids—possibly suffering from 'health illiteracy'—might always choose the less healthy option. This can lead to further considerations: some institutions might want to allow food options but only those that have beneficial nutritional values. Hence there is scope for more than sufficientarian options by attempting to enhance health as much as possible. I do not think that such a policy would be unjust, although it raises other concerns regarding the possible manipulation of choice. Be that as it may, sufficientarianism, in contrast, would aim at a sufficient level of nutrition and making school meals a pleasant experience for all children. It would not aim at the best possible nutritional outcome of school meals.

Screening programs, which are often used as public-health measures, are more complex cases. Strategies to encourage citizens, especially high-risk groups, to enrol in these programs can differ enormously in their intensity. If worried citizens would not be able to participate at all in these precautionary measures for financial reasons, despite the potential severity of a detectable disease, this would be reason to argue that they cannot feel a part of a society. After all, not being able to tackle such health-related worries implies that society apparently sees poor people's health and their fears as of minor importance. Accordingly, access to such screening programs for each citizen seems to be required by a sufficientarian account of public health, though not any level of such provision—for instance, on the level of medical surveillance a rich and worried person might choose. Also, attempts to compulsively guarantee full and incessant health-related information to all citizens or to manipulate less worried—some would say careless—citizens into enrolling on such programs is a different matter, and it is not justified on a sufficientarian basis.

So far, I have offered a brief explanation of the general aim of sufficientarianism, which is, to my mind, the inclusion of all in society. Everybody should be a member of society, and no citizen should feel excluded. There is also a requirement for a 'currency' of sufficientarianism about health: we have to determine in what way we should assess the level of enough health for all. In the following, I would like to explore in greater detail what the criteria could be for cashing out sufficientarianism about health. This can further help in restricting the proper scope of public-health interventions.

As I have explained in the second chapter of the book, we cannot directly target the health of people by public-health measures. Rather, these instruments aim at the causes of the causes of disease—and hence at dispositional aspects of the health status of people. Public health is mainly concerned with the circumstances of choices that might have an impact on health. I have said earlier that one such circumstance is having information about the possible consequences of certain lifestyles, about health threats due to habits such as smoking, inadequate diet, and so on. Other circumstances include being able to access recreational activities or to avoid permanent stress, noise, darkness, dampness, pollution, and so on. A general description of the goal of public health might therefore be that it aims at providing the necessary means for everyone to be able to make healthy choices, not to actually make people healthy. The level of individual health that citizens pursue, how fit, for instance, they want to be, is up to them.

The threshold we would probably consider first when thinking about a restriction of public-health measures is the traditional medical notion of health as the absence of disease. After all, this is a minimal notion of health, as I have explained in an earlier chapter. Yet, since public health aims at health dispositions, not at health directly, almost every change in the circumstances of choice might decrease the risk of disease. So, even if the avoidance of disease is our aim—which looks like a minimalist goal—we have not, in virtue of targeting the circumstances of risks for disease, restricted the scope of intervention after all.

One way forward for sufficientarianism about public health will be to acknowledge the value of health as an element—but only one element—of a decent life. There are low levels of health that are perfectly in congruence with living a decent life, and there are risks of disease that are worth taking because of other aspects of living a good life. Health is not usually our only or even our major concern when contemplating how to live.

Hence we are thrown back to the more general notion of the conditions of a decent life. Sufficientarianism ought to cash out this idea in a minimalist sense. I have most of the time used 'decent life' instead of 'good life' to allude to the minimalist agenda. Now, a decent life seems at least to require the ability to fulfil basic needs. Accordingly, this might be the starting point for introducing a currency of sufficientarianism. Indeed, I believe that the most promising way forward for sufficientarianism is by considering the concept of need. Admittedly, the concept of need is not very popular in ethics and political philosophy. Many deem it too flexible to tell us anything of significance about the decent life. It seems that every fancy wish seems to be a suitable candidate for becoming a need. I believe this worry to be wrong, and I will briefly discuss the significant difference between desires and needs. In addition, needs seem to be the proper candidate for our concern here, because they usually come along with a powerful claim. After all, we are concerned here with issues of social justice—or what we owe to each other. If we say that we need something, we express that its provision is urgent, that we cannot do without it. We therefore refer to a potentially or already harmful situation.

Basic needs are absolute in that their determination does not require interpersonal comparison. Human beings have basic needs by virtue of the fact that they are persons. If these needs cannot be fulfilled, then persons suffer serious harm. It is implied that not every disease is posing a threat to basic health-related needs. This idea stands in contrast to popular theories, such as Norman Daniels's, which see requirements to the maintenance and restoration of (negative) health—that is, the absence of all disease—as instances of health-care needs.

I submit that health care, including public health, should aim at providing the necessary means for being able to fulfil basic health-related needs. In order to discuss such absolute, basic needs of people, we should be clearer about the distinction between instrumental and basic, or fundamental, needs. First, here is a general analysis of the concept of need: A needs X in order to φ. Note that there can be nonnormative usages of *need*. For example: 'In order to conduct electricity an element needs a free electron'[11]. I am interested in the normative use only, since I want to highlight the connection between need and living a decent life. The nonnormative use lacks the practical necessity I am interested in, which is the urgency of the claim. In contrast, people want to express that there is something harmful happening to them when they are seriously ill. Hence we use the term *need* normatively when we say 'I need to be minimally healthy'.

With the help of the general definition of claims of need, we can now distinguish instrumental from fundamental needs. An instrumental need depends on the specific, possibly idiosyncratic, goals and aims of the person in question, while a fundamental need is not derived from such specific aspects. For instance, a person might say, 'I need £100 to buy that coat', but it is a need that depends on her having the aim to use the coat for a particular purpose. It is possible to challenge the actual need for that coat. The money is just necessary for the goal—to get the coat—but the achievement of the goal itself is not necessarily something needed. The person in the example would have to explain why she needs the coat. To answer the question why a person needs X is to say something about the normative significance of the goal φ, where X is a necessary condition of its achievement. The goal could be seen as always referring to an aspect of well-being, but where needs gain urgency, I submit, is where something is needed to prevent harm; it is therefore putting forward a negative perspective, focusing on the avoidance and elimination of harm. This justification of needs can go on until it reaches a point where one cannot give any further reference to a more basic goal, such as protection from cold, but only assert that one just cannot do without it—that is, that one will be seriously harmed without X. Therefore, these needs are fundamental or basic needs.

Instances of health-related serious absolute harms are severe illnesses. I have already said that not every disease equals an impairment of the ability to live a decent life. But otherwise what kinds of diseases constitute serious harms might differ between persons: A farmer, for instance, might deem hay fever to be a serious impairment, since her ability to work in her business is compromised by this condition, whereas others might not be much affected in their ability to live a decent life. In contrast to this variability of normative assessment, if someone has an illness that involves a fundamental threat to survival, an impairment of basic abilities, or severe pain and agony, people will immediately understand her claim of need (and they usually believe it to require an explanation when someone in this situation does not claim to be in need). So there seems to be a difference between cases like the farmer with hay fever and indisputable cases of basic health-related need. While in the latter case everyone would agree that there is a need for restoration of health, or at least for the best possible compensation of the impairment, this does not hold for the former case. These considerations show that health-care institutions need to be careful not to miss or misinterpret health needs. In the history of medicine there are numerous examples of how health needs can be misinterpreted—for instance, when the need of paraplegic people was seen to consist of being able to walk instead of being mobile.

This analysis shows that needs are not due to desires, not even to very strong desires. A desire is intentional; a need is not intentional. That is to say that the content of a desire depends on a mental act directed on an object, while a need depends on a state of the world. If a person, for instance, needs something in order to get rid of a terrible headache, then both aspirin and ibuprofen will work as means to fulfil the need, even if the person does not even know that both substances are painkillers or desperately wants to take aspirin but not ibuprofen. Hence what satisfies a need is independent of mental attitudes, whereas what fulfils a desire is not always a separate issue.

Sufficientarianism about health-related needs would probably best start with serious diseases that affect everyone. But it should not restrict its scope in a way that excludes the possible justification of individual basic health-related needs. For the purposes of general health care it is therefore plausible to aim at providing for the treatment of almost all possible diseases. Yet when it comes to public-health measures, there need to be further concerns: First, since public health does not deal directly with the treatment of disease but with risks to being affected by disease, and since it operates on a population level, sufficientarianism about public health would further need an assessment of the severity of risks to citizens generally. It would probably come up with a list of 'big killers', such as heart and lung disease and cancer, and the most frequent severely disabling conditions, such as strokes and head injuries. In fact, these are of course already some of the main targets of public-health interventions. Second, especially because public-health measures aim at causes of causes, interventions require an assessment of the benefits of lowering risks in relation to the possible harms that are not related to health but to other basic needs of human beings, such as people's need to be free to decide for themselves or having access to pleasurable goods. Obviously, not every improvement of health disposition is worth the effort. This is not only meant economically but also, more importantly, in terms of the costs for citizens' ability to live a decent life. As I have stressed before, health is not their only concern.

Sufficientarianism in public health should be modest in its aims and only promote the provision of necessary means for general health-related basic needs. Obviously there is a lot of scope for disagreement about what this minimum requires in terms of actual public provisions. Such disagreement is mostly a political issue that cannot be decided by philosophical analysis. Sufficientarianism in public health should also always consider other basic needs of people and how they might be affected by public-health policies. This requires balancing of different possible policies and a public debate about the relative importance of values such as health, security and individual liberty. Again, there is little that philosophy or a theory of social justice alone can contribute to such a question. My goal in this part of the chapter has been to show the normative benefits of sufficientarianism regarding health justice, especially in restricting state action to the provision of enabling conditions, and also to analyse the currency in which such a sufficientarian theory can be fleshed out. In respect to the latter task, I have merely been able to offer initial thoughts regarding the concept of health-related basic needs. A more thorough analysis would require much more detail and also a comparison to alternative theories.

It should be emphasised yet again that sufficientarianism is a version of a theory of social justice; it is concerned with what we owe each other. Citizens might decide, in political processes, that they would like to grant each other more than what justice requires. This would be a political decision made by a political sovereign. My argument was only to claim that societies that do not fulfil the minimum requirement of providing the necessary means for inclusion of all citizens fail on normative grounds. My reasoning does not exclude provisions that, for instance, aim at greater health equality or an improvement of the health of the citizenry over and above the avoidance of significant disease. Yet such further provisions are not imperative on grounds of a theory of social justice.

HOW OUGHT WE RATION MEDICAL RESOURCES?

So far, my considerations on justified claims in health care have not been influenced by concerns regarding any recent crisis in health-care provision. It has been an examination of justice under idealised conditions. It seems clear that, from my point of view, treatment of minor diseases, and medical services that do not deal with present or likely future pathological states at all, do not generate entitlements. However, we know that even if legitimate demands in my theory are more limited than they are according to other theories of justice, it is still highly unlikely that every claim justified on the combined theory of naturalism and sufficientarianism can be fulfilled under current conditions of scarcity. Therefore, we need further considerations of justice, which ultimately ought to lead to a valid model of rationing.

Yet again it can be seen that the specific amount of actual scarcity of goods is, at least in the case of health care, a variable, which is highly influenced by political and societal decisions. After all, societies could of course fund all health-care resources required so that every health-care claim that has been justified under idealised conditions could actually be fulfilled. But this is not desirable, because societies also have other political aims, such as education or culture and the arts, that they would like to support by public funds. Hence it is unlikely that any state would supply health care with enough means, where 'enough' is specified by the resources necessary to treat all harmful dysfunctions.

To develop a theory of just rationing, the first question to ask from the perspective defended in this chapter would be which diseases cause noncomparative harm. These constitute the sphere of justified claims. As we have seen, this question is answered without further ado both for normativism and egalitarianism. Every disease would count either as disadvantage or as harm by definition. This is wrong, according to my theory. Under nonideal conditions it would, second, be necessary to restrict entitlements even further. This is what is usually called rationing—that is, the rejection of claims that would be regarded as justified under more favourable conditions. Rationing itself, of course, ought to lead to a just distribution of the actually available resources. I want to spend the rest of the chapter dealing with this problem of rationing from a sufficientarian point of view.

I believe that rationing should be carried out by a ranking of diseases according to their significance in terms of well-being, broadly conceived.

This can only be achieved by collective effort. Additionally, there need to be comparisons of the costs of different treatments. As we have seen in an earlier chapter, this kind of evaluation is not unheard-of, although the methodology of common cost-effectiveness analysis can be improved. In contrast to many health-care economists, I believe that especially high-cost treatments ought to be publicly funded because it is then that we usually need to rely on the solidarity of our fellow citizens. The less grave in terms of absolute harm and the less expensive a specific treatment is, the more justified it is to cut its collective funding and transfer it into a scheme of individual provision.

It seems obvious that the naturalist theory of disease cannot help with the task of evaluating diseases in terms of their grade of harm. Naturalism fulfils its task by restricting entitlements to impairments of functional abilities and curtailing pathologisation and medicalisation. What we further need is a theory of well-being and harm, which cannot be fully developed in this book. However, the evaluation and eventually the ranking of these pathological conditions might, yet again, gain from a naturalist theory of disease, because the grade of harm involved with a certain disease does not seem to be completely unrelated to the functions affected. Generally speaking we could say that the higher or more complex an affected organismic function is, the more serious the harm, because higher organismic functions, such as mobility, memory or cognition, can be considered foundational in terms of a decent life for human beings.

Nevertheless, although this relationship between natural functions and the good for human beings may even constitute a basis for an objective theory of minimal well-being, it seems obvious that collective considerations and evaluations need to be involved. How to ration collectively funded health care is ultimately a communal and political task.

CONCLUSION

In this chapter I have defended a combination of a naturalist theory of disease and a specific theory of justice, sufficientarianism, which argues for a provision of goods necessary for the chance to lead a decent life. Health justice, according to this combined approach, means that everyone ought to be entitled to the treatment of noncomparatively harmful dysfunctions. If this is not possible for reasons of shortage of resources, then health-care resources should be rationed in relation to their significance for the well-being of patients and to their costs of treatment.

Sufficientarianism provides an important benefit in restricting the aims of state action, as it endorses a minimal conception of justice. In virtue of setting such limits to state action, it is a minimalist theory of civil and human rights. An expansion of such obligations might be achieved in real political processes, but I do not believe that an expansive scope of individual rights—for instance, to the best possible health-promoting living conditions—can be justified by normative theory.

Sufficientarianism is also useful in respect to public measures aimed at health promotion. Public-health policies are difficult to assess in terms of their outcomes and success. They are notoriously contested in many societies in terms of their impact on people's lives and choices, even where these are allegedly enabling citizens to live a decent life. Public-health interventions should not only be restricted in scope and intensity for reasons of sufficiency per se but also because health ought to be seen as part of a wider context of welfare provision in liberal societies. Other aspects of welfare provision, especially securing individual liberty and self-determination, might compromise the legitimacy of health policies.

As a final caveat, it should be admitted that I have almost exclusively developed my argument against the backdrop of seeing health as something of intrinsic value—that is, as avoiding absolute harm. At the same time, I have accepted that health can also be seen as an asset. If we interpret society as a site of competition between citizens—which in many countries, up to a point, is a fitting description of reality—we might need to consider more aspects of comparative health justice. Here the plausibility of sufficientarianism might come to an end.

Further Reading

This section is meant to advise readers who would like to delve deeper into the topics covered in different chapters of the book. There are numerous problems with achieving that aim which should be mentioned: First, health justice is a subject involving several disciplines; hence it is difficult to not get lost in a sea of publications. Still, it is not sufficient—when performing your own research—to only look for literature on otherwise very helpful disciplinary websites, such as PhilPapers or The Philosopher's Index. Second, most of the relevant literature is scattered in edited collections and journals. I have aimed at listing mainly edited collections that contain numerous valuable readings and monographs. There is, of course, much more to explore. The websites just mentioned might help you start your own search. Third, students these days tend to restrict their research to sources that are available online. In addition, they and even experienced scholars in the field tend to believe that publications that are more than, say, ten years old are ancient and out-of-date. This is not adequate. Proper scientific research requires physically visiting libraries and considering older publications. However, it should be acknowledged that books, especially those out of print, are not available for all scholars globally. I have therefore aimed at listing mainly easily available literature.

CHAPTER 1

The debate on the concept of disease has a long history. For an overview, see my 'Classic Concepts of Disease', published in the *International Encyclopedia of Public Health*, edited by Kris Heggenhougen and Stella R. Quah (Academic, 2008). The concept of disease has been more thoroughly discussed from the perspective of philosophy since roughly the 1970s. There are numerous helpful handbooks and encyclopaedias available on topics in the philosophy of medicine. *The Bloomsbury Companion to Contemporary Philosophy of Medicine*, edited by James A. Marcum (Bloomsbury, 2016); *The Routledge Companion to Philosophy of Medicine*, edited by Miriam Solomon, Jeremy R. Simon and Harold Kincaid (Routledge, 2017); and the *Handbook of the Philosophy of Medicine*, edited by Thomas Schramme and Steven Edwards (Springer, 2016). *The Nature of Disease* by Lawrie Reznek is an immensely helpful study (Routledge, 1987). The best out-of-print anthology that focuses on the concepts of health and disease is *Concepts of Health and Disease: Interdisciplinary Perspectives*, edited by Arthur L. Caplan, H Tristram Engelhardt Jr. and James McCartney (Addison-Wesley, 1981). Arthur L. Caplan, James McCartney and Dominic A. Sisti have also edited *Health, Disease, and Illness: Concepts in Medicine* (Georgetown University Press, 2004). Finally, an important collection of essays is *What Is Disease?* This book was edited by James M. Humber and Robert F. Almeder (Humana Press, 1997). A philosophical study on the concept of illness is S. Kay Toombs's *The Meaning of Illness: A Phenomenological Account of the Different Perspectives of Physician and Patient* (Kluwer, 1992). A more recent study is *Illness: The Cry of the Flesh* by Havi Carel (Routledge, 2018).

CHAPTER 2

There is considerable overlap with the further reading section for the first chapter. An invaluable monograph specifically on the concept of health is Lennart Nordenfelt's *On the Nature of Health: An Action-Theoretic Approach* (Kluwer, 1995). Nordenfelt has published many more articles and books that I would recommend the reader to explore. The WHO's definition of *health* is found in their constitution, which is available on the institution's website at http://apps.who.int/gb/bd/PDF/bd47/EN/constitution-en.pdf. The public-health perspective has been introduced to a wider audience by Michael Gideon Marmot in his book *Status Syndrome: How Your Social Standing Directly Affects Your Health* (Bloomsbury, 2004). Another important social epidemiologist is Richard G. Wilkinson. An accessible work of his, cowritten with Kate Pickett, is *The Spirit Level: Why Equality Makes Societies Stronger* (Bloomsbury, 2010). The more specialised debate on grades of health can be found in journal articles by Dan Hausman ('Valuing Health', *Philosophy & Public Affairs*, 2006) and Andrew S. Schroeder ('Rethinking Health: Health or Healthier Than?' *The British Journal for the Philosophy of Science*, 2013).

CHAPTER 3

The philosophical literature on social justice is vast. A good starting point is Adam Swift's *Political Philosophy: A Beginner's Guide for Students and Politicians* (Polity, 2001). Political philosophers tend to say that the modern debate on social justice started with John Rawls's extremely important *A Theory of Justice*, originally published in 1971 (Harvard University Press, 1999). But there were numerous important publications predating Rawls, and he of course also started his work before the seventies. Important earlier authors include Leonard Hobhouse, Friedrich Hayek, D. Daiches Raphael, Richard Titmuss and Alan John Mitchell Milne. Robert Nozick initiated the modern version of libertarianism in his *Anarchy, State, and Utopia* (Basic Books, 1974). There have hardly been any publications by libertarians on health justice specifically, though Tristram Engelhardt Jr. and Jan Narveson should be mentioned as proponents.

The taxonomy of the modern scholarly debate has been heavily influenced by Derek Parfit's distinction between egalitarianism and prioritarianism, which was first put forward in his Lindley Lecture, 'Equality or Priority' (University of Kansas, 1995). Later, sufficientarianism entered as a third type of theory, although the idea itself predates the coinage of the labels. A helpful introduction that covers all three theories is Iwao Hirose's *Egalitarianism* (Routledge, 2015). The basic idea of luck egalitarianism is usually credited to Ronald Dworkin. His main thoughts on this topic are collected in his *Sovereign Virtue* (Harvard University Press, 2000). Relational egalitarianism had one of its first defenders in Elizabeth S. Anderson ('What Is the Point of Equality?' *Ethics*, 1999). Another influential author in this vein is Iris Marion Young, starting with her *Justice and the Politics of Difference* (Princeton University Press, 1990).

Liam Shields's study *Just Enough: Sufficiency as a Demand of Justice* (Edinburgh University Press, 2016) is an important contribution to sufficientarianism. Another interesting contribution is George Sher's *Equality for Inegalitarians* (Cambridge University Press, 2014). I have myself developed a sufficientarian theory of social justice in my book (only available in German) *Gerechtigkeit und soziale Praxis* [Justice and social practice] (Frankfurt: Campus, 2006). The 'currency' terminology for metrics of justice is due to Gerald A. Cohen ('On the Currency of Egalitarian Justice', *Ethics*, 1989).

CHAPTER 4

The most influential philosophical theory of health justice has been developed by Norman Daniels. He has published two major monographs (and more on tangential topics, such as justice for the elderly): *Just Health Care*

(Cambridge University Press, 1985) and *Just Health: Meeting Health Needs Fairly* (Cambridge University Press, 2008). Jennifer Prah Ruger's book *Health and Social Justice* (Oxford University Press, 2010) argues from the perspective of the capabilities approach. Similarly, Sridhar Venkatapuram, in his *Health Justice* (Polity, 2011) develops an argument for a capability of being healthy as the main currency of health justice. A theory that leans towards sufficientarianism is *Social Justice: The Moral Foundations of Public Health and Health Policy* by Madison Powers and Ruth Faden (Oxford University Press, 2006). Shlomi Segall's *Health, Luck, and Justice* (Princeton University Press, 2009) is a thorough study from a luck-egalitarian point of view. Another important contribution to health justice, which I have not directly discussed in the chapter, is Lawrence C. Becker's *Habilitation, Health, and Agency: A Framework for Basic Justice* (Oxford University Press, 2012). Allen E. Buchanan's selected essays, *Justice and Health Care* (Oxford University Press, 2009), is also to be recommended, as well as Yvonne Denier's study *Efficiency, Justice and Care: Philosophical Reflections on Scarcity in Health Care* (Springer, 2007.)

Daniel Hausman's *Valuing Health: Well-Being, Freedom, and Suffering* (Oxford University Press, 2015) is a very valuable contribution to the philosophy and economics of health. Greg Bognar and Iwao Hirose published an accessible textbook on the thorny issue of restricting access to health-care resources: *The Ethics of Health Care Rationing: An Introduction* (Routledge, 2014). Finally, an important collection of essays is *Medicine and Social Justice: Essays on the Distribution of Health Care*, edited by Rosamond Rhodes, Margaret P. Battin and Anita Silvers (Oxford University Press, 2012).

CHAPTER 5

John Rawls's book *The Law of Peoples* (Harvard University Press, 1999) ignited a debate in political philosophy on global justice, which has led to an enormous amount of publications. An accessible introduction to relevant issues is Mathias Risse's book *On Global Justice* (Princeton University Press, 2012). Gillian Brock has defended a cosmopolitan perspective in *Global Justice: A Cosmopolitan Account* (Oxford University Press, 2009). An important book defending a weaker version of cosmopolitanism that includes elements of statism is David Miller's *Strangers in Our Midst: The Political Philosophy of Immigration* (Harvard University Press, 2016).

The discussion on health inequalities is mainly led in public health. Margaret Whitehead's publications have been influential in the normative debate within social epidemiology. She has published numerous studies and reports. Probably the best place to begin is her article 'The Concepts and Principles of Equity and Health' (*International Journal of Health Services*, 1992). From a philosophical perspective, Sudhir Anand, Fabienne Peter and Amartya Sen's anthology *Public Health, Ethics, and Equity* (Oxford University Press, 2004) is very valuable. A helpful introduction to the debate on the right to health from the perspective of political philosophy is *The Human Right to Health* by Jonathan Wolff (Norton, 2012).

There have not been many publications specifically on global health justice, but good places to start are the monograph *Global Health Justice and Governance* by Jennifer Prah Ruger (Oxford University Press, 2018) and the collections *Health Inequalities and Global Justice*, edited by Patti Tamara Lenard and Christine Straehle (Edinburgh University Press, 2012), as well as *Global Health and Global Health Ethics*, edited by Solomon R. Benatar and Gillian Brock (Cambridge University Press, 2011). An anthology specifically focusing on migrants is *Migration, Health and Inequality*, edited by Felicity Thomas and Jasmine Gideon (Zed Books, 2013).

CHAPTER 6

The ideas of pathologisation, medicalisation and healthisation can be studied in Peter Conrad's *The Medicalization of Society: On the Transformation of Human Conditions into Treatable Disorder*s (Johns Hopkins University Press, 2007). A powerful critique of modern medicine is *The Tyranny of Health: Doctors and the Regulation of Lifestyles* by Michael Fitzpatrick (Routledge, 2001). An interesting sociological account is Nikolas S. Rose's *The Politics of Life Itself: Biomedicine, Power, and Subjectivity in the Twenty-First Century* (Princeton University Press, 2007). Another valuable contribution to the social contexts of health care is Alan Cribb's *Health and the Good Society: Setting Healthcare Ethics in Social Context* (Oxford University Press, 2005).

The debate on goals of medicine was pursued in the important study *A Philosophical Basis of Medical Practice: Toward a Philosophy and Ethic of the Healing Professions*, by Edmund D. Pellegrino and David C. Thomasma (Oxford University Press, 1981). Another relevant work is Leon Kass's *Toward a More Natural Science: Biology and Human Affairs* (Free Press, 1985). The Hastings Center's report is published in the anthology *The Goals of Medicine: The Forgotten Issue in Health Care Reform*, edited by Mark J. Hanson and Daniel Callahan (Georgetown University Press, 1999).

CHAPTER 7

What Is Enough? Sufficiency, Justice, and Health, edited by Carina Fourie and Annette Rid (Oxford University Press, 2017) is the best place to start exploring sufficientarian perspectives specifically in health justice.

The philosophical problems surrounding disability and possible forms of harm are discussed in *Disability and Disadvantage*, edited by Kimberley Brownlee and Adam Cureton (Oxford University Press, 2009) and in *Disability and the Good Human Life*, edited by Jerome E. Bickenbach, Franziska Felder and Barbara Schmidtz (Cambridge University Press, 2014).

The idea of health literacy, including its political agenda, can be studied in Ilona Kickbusch's editorial 'Health Literacy: Engaging in a Political Debate' (*International Journal of Public Health*, 2009).

Thomas H. Marshall's influential account of the development of rights in welfare states is published in a book titled after his long essay 'Citizenship and Social Class' (Cambridge University Press, 1950).

A valuable monograph on the concept of need is *Needs* by Garrett Thomson (Routledge, 1987). A more recent collection of essays is edited by Soran Reader, *The Philosophy of Need* (Cambridge University Press, 2005).

Bibliography

Anand, Sudhir, Fabienne Peter and Amartya Sen, eds. *Public Health, Ethics, and Equity*. Oxford; New York: Oxford University Press, 2004.

Anderson, Elizabeth S. 'What Is the Point of Equality?' *Ethics* 109, no. 2 (Jan. 1999): 287–337.

Becker, Lawrence C. *Habilitation, Health, and Agency: A Framework for Basic Justice*. New York: Oxford University Press, 2012.

Benatar, Solomon R., and Gillian Brock, eds. *Global Health and Global Health Ethics*. Cambridge Medicine. Cambridge; New York: Cambridge University Press, 2011.

Beauchamp, D. E. 'Public Health: III. Philosophy'. In *Encyclopedia of Bioethics*, 3rd ed., edited by Stephen G. Post, 2210–15. New York: Macmillan Reference, 1995.

Bickenbach, Jerome E., Franziska Felder and Barbara Schmitz. *Disability and the Good Human Life*. Cambridge Disability Law and Policy Series. New York: Cambridge University Press, 2014.

Bognar, Greg, and Iwao Hirose. *The Ethics of Health Care Rationing: An Introduction*. London; New York: Routledge, Taylor & Francis Group, 2014.

Boorse, Christopher. 'Health as a Theoretical Concept'. *Philosophy of Science* 44, no. 4 (1977): 542–73.

Brandt, Richard B. *A Theory of the Good and the Right*. Oxford; New York: Clarendon Press; Oxford University Press, 1979.

Brock, Gillian. *Global Justice: A Cosmopolitan Account*. Oxford; New York: Oxford University Press, 2009.

Brownlee, Kimberley, and Adam Cureton, eds. *Disability and Disadvantage*. Oxford; New York: Oxford University Press, 2009.

Buchanan, Allen, Dan W. Brock, Norman Daniels and Daniel Wikler. *From Chance to Choice: Genetics and Justice*. Cambridge; New York: Cambridge University Press, 2000.

Buchanan, Allen E. *Justice and Health Care: Selected Essays*. New York: Oxford University Press, 2009.

Caplan, Arthur L., H. Tristram Engelhardt Jr. and James J. McCartney. *Concepts of Health and Disease: Interdisciplinary Perspectives*. Reading, MA: Addison-Wesley, Advanced Book Program/World Science Division, 1981.

Caplan, Arthur L., James J. McCartney and Dominic A. Sisti, eds. *Health, Disease, and Illness: Concepts in Medicine*. Washington, DC: Georgetown University Press, 2004.

Carel, Havi. *Illness: The Cry of the Flesh*. 3rd ed. Milton Park, Abingdon, Oxon; New York: Routledge, 2018.

Clouser, K. Danner, Charles M. Culver and Bernard Gert. 'Malady'. In *What Is Disease?*, Biomedical Ethics Reviews, edited by James M. Humber and Robert F. Almeder, 173–217. Totowa, NJ: Humana Press, 1997.

Cohen, Gerald A. 'On the Currency of Egalitarian Justice'. *Ethics* 99, no. 4 (1989): 906–44. Available online at http://www.mit.edu/~shaslang/mprg/GACohenCEJ.pdf.

Conrad, Peter. 'Medicalization and Social Control'. *Annual Review of Sociology* 18 (1992): 209–32.

———. *The Medicalization of Society: On the Transformation of Human Conditions into Treatable Disorders*. Baltimore, MD: Johns Hopkins University Press, 2007.

Cooper, Rachel. 'Disease'. *Studies in History and Philosophy of Science Part C: Studies in History and Philosophy of Biological and Biomedical Sciences* 33, no. 2 (2002): 263–82.

Cribb, Alan. *Health and the Good Society: Setting Healthcare Ethics in Social Context*. Issues in Biomedical Ethics. Oxford; New York: Clarendon Press; Oxford University Press, 2005.

Daniels, Norman. *Just Health Care*. Studies in Philosophy and Health Policy. Cambridge [Cambridgeshire]; New York: Cambridge University Press, 1985.

———. *Just Health: Meeting Health Needs Fairly*. Cambridge; New York: Cambridge University Press, 2008.

———. 'Wide Reflective Equilibrium and Theory Acceptance in Ethics'. *Journal of Philosophy* 76, no. 5 (1979): 256–82.

Denier, Yvonne. *Efficiency, Justice and Care: Philosophical Reflections on Scarcity in Health Care*. International Library of Ethics, Law, and the New Medicine, 33. Dordrecht, Holland: Springer, 2007.

Dworkin, Ronald. *Sovereign Virtue: The Theory and Practice of Equality*. Cambridge, MA: Harvard University Press, 2000.

Ebert, Roger. 'Sundance #3: Of Heart and Humor'. Festivals & Awards. RogerEbert.com. 7 August 2005. http://rogerebert.suntimes.com/apps/pbcs.dll/article?AID=/20050125/FILMFESTIVALS05/501250301/1023.

Engelhardt, H. Tristram, Jr. 'The Concepts of Health and Disease'. In *Evaluation and Explanation in the Biomedical Sciences: Proceedings of the First Trans-disciplinary Symposium on Philosophy and Medicine, Held at Galveston, May 9–11, 1974*, Philosophy and Medicine, vol.1, edited by H. Tristram Engelhardt Jr. and Stuart F. Spicker, 125–141. Dordrecht, Holland; Boston: Reidel Pub. Co., 1975.

———. *The Foundations of Bioethics*. 2nd ed. New York: Oxford University Press, 1996.

Farber, Seth. *Madness, Heresy, and the Rumor of Angels: The Revolt against the Mental Health System*. Chicago: Open Court, 1993.

Feinberg, Joel. 'Noncomparative Justice'. *The Philosophical Review* 83, no. 3 (1974): 297–338.

Fitzpatrick, Michael. *The Tyranny of Health: Doctors and the Regulation of Lifestyle*. London; New York: Routledge, 2001.

Fourie, Carina, and Annette Rid, eds. *What Is Enough? Sufficiency, Justice, and Health*. Oxford; New York: Oxford University Press, 2017.

Frankfurt, Harry. 'Equality as a Moral Ideal'. *Ethics* 98, no. 1 (Oct. 1987): 21–43.

Hanson, Mark J., and Daniel Callahan, eds. *The Goals of Medicine: The Forgotten Issue in Health Care Reform*. Hastings Center Studies in Ethics. Washington, DC: Georgetown University Press, 1999.

Harris, John. 'Is There a Coherent Social Conception of Disability?' *J Med Ethics* 26, no. 2 (Apr. 2000): 95–100. https://jme.bmj.com/content/26/2/95.

Hausman, Daniel M. 'Valuing Health'. *Philosophy & Public Affairs* 34, no. 3 (Sum. 2006): 246–74.

———. *Valuing Health: Well-Being, Freedom, and Suffering*. Population-Level Bioethics Series. Oxford; New York: Oxford University Press, 2015.

Hirose, Iwao. *Egalitarianism*. New Problems of Philosophy. London; New York: Routledge, 2015.

Honneth, Axel. *Freedom's Right: The Social Foundations of Democratic Life*. Cambridge: Polity Press, 2014.

Humber, James M., and Robert F. Almeder, eds. *What Is Disease?* Biomedical Ethics Reviews. Totowa, NJ: Humana Press, 1997.

Hume, David. *Enquiries Concerning Human Understanding and Concerning the Principles of Morals*. 3d ed. Introduction, comparative table of contents and analytical index by L. A. Selby-Bigge, and text rev. and notes by P. H. Nidditch. Oxford: Clarendon Press, 1975.

Kass, Leon. *Toward a More Natural Science: Biology and Human Affairs*. New York: Free Press, 1985.

Kickbusch, Ilona. 'Health Literacy: Engaging in a Political Debate'. *Int J Public Health* 54, no. 3 (2009): 131–32.

Lenard, Patti Tamara, and Christine Straehle, eds. *Health Inequalities and Global Justice*. Edinburgh: Edinburgh University Press, 2012.

Marcum, James A., ed. *The Bloomsbury Companion to Contemporary Philosophy of Medicine*. Bloomsbury Companions. London; New York: Bloomsbury Academic, an imprint of Bloomsbury Publishing Plc, 2016.

Marmot, Michael Gideon. *Status Syndrome: How Your Social Standing Directly Affects Your Health and Life Expectancy*. London: Bloomsbury Publishing, 2004.

Marshall, Thomas H. *Citizenship and Social Class, and Other Essays*. Cambridge: Cambridge University Press, 1950.

Mergenthaler, Daniela. 'Medicine as Task—Karl E. Rothschuh's Philosophy of Medicine'. *Medicine, Health Care and Philosophy* 7, no. 3 (2005): 253–60.

Miller, David. *Principles of Social Justice*. Cambridge, MA: Harvard University Press, 1999.

———. *Strangers in Our Midst: The Political Philosophy of Immigration*. Cambridge, MA: Harvard University Press, 2016.

Nordenfelt, Lennart. *On the Nature of Health: An Action-Theoretic Approach*. Philosephy and Medicine, vol. 26. 2nd rev. and enl. ed. Dordrecht, Holland; Boston: Kluwer, 1995.

Nozick, Robert. *Anarchy, State, and Utopia*. New York: Basic Books, 1974.

Nuffield Council on Bioethics. *Public Health: Ethical Issues*. Cambridge: Cambridge Publishers, 2007.

Parfit, Derek. *Equality or Priority?* The Lindley Lecture. [Kansas]: University of Kansas, 1995.

Parsons, Talcott. 'The Sick Role and the Role of the Physician Reconsidered'. *Milbank Memorial Fund Quarterly: Health and Society* 53, no. 3 (Feb. 1975): 257–78.

Pellegrino, Edmund D., and David C. Thomasma. *A Philosophical Basis of Medical Practice: Toward a Philosophy and Ethic of the Healing Professions*. New York: Oxford University Press, 1981.

Pellegrino, Edmund D. 'The Goals and Ends of Medicine: How Are They to Be Defined?' In *The Goals of Medicine: The Forgotten Issue in Health Care Reform*, edited by Mark J. Hanson and Daniel Callahan, 55–68. Hastings Center Studies in Ethics. Washington, DC: Georgetown University Press, 1999.

Powers, Madison, and Ruth Faden. *Social Justice: The Moral Foundations of Public Health and Health Policy*. Issues in Biomedical Ethics. Oxford; New York: Oxford University Press, 2006.

Rawls, John. 'The Independence of Moral Theory'. *Proceedings and Addresses of the American Philosophical Association* 48 (1974–1975): 5–22.

———. *Justice as Fairness: A Restatement*. Edited by Erin Kelly. Cambridge, MA: Harvard University Press, 2001.

———. *The Law of Peoples; with, the Idea of Public Reason Revisited*. Cambridge, MA: Harvard University Press, 1999.

———. *A Theory of Justice*. Rev. ed. Cambridge, MA: Belknap Press of Harvard University Press, 1999. First published 1971.

Reader, Soran, ed. *The Philosophy of Need*. Royal Institute of Philosophy Supplement, 57. Cambridge; New York: Cambridge University Press, 2005.

Reznek, Lawrie. *The Nature of Disease*. Philosophical Issues in Science. London; New York: Routledge & Kegan Paul, 1987.

Rhodes, Rosamond, Margaret P. Battin and Anita Silvers, eds. *Medicine and Social Justice: Essays on the Distribution of Health Care*. Oxford; New York: Oxford University Press, 2002.

Risse, Mathias. *On Global Justice*. Princeton: Princeton University Press, 2012.

Rose, Nikolas S. *Politics of Life Itself: Biomedicine, Power, and Subjectivity in the Twenty-First Century*. Information Series. Princeton: Princeton University Press, 2007.
Ruger, Jennifer Prah. *Global Health Justice and Governance*. New product edition. New York: Oxford University Press, 2018.
Rothschuh, Karl E. 'Der Krankheitsbegriff (Was ist Krankheit?)'. *Hippokrates* 43 (1972): 3–17.
———. *Health and Social Justice*. Oxford; New York: Oxford University Press, 2010.
'Classic Concepts of Disease'. In *International Encyclopedia of Public Health*, vol. 1 of 6, edited by Kris Heggenhougen and Stella R. Quah, 726–33. Oxford: Academic, 2008.
———. *Gerechtigkeit und soziale Praxis* [Justice and social practice]. Frankfurt: Campus, 2006.
Schramme, Thomas, and Steven Edwards, eds. *Handbook of the Philosophy of Medicine*. New York: Springer Berlin Heidelberg, 2016.
Schroeder, S. Andrew. 'Rethinking Health: Healthy or Healthier Than?' *The British Journal for the Philosophy of Science* 64, no. 1 (Mar. 2013): 131–59.
Sedgwick, Peter. 'Illness: Mental and Otherwise', *The Hastings Center Studies* 1, no. 3, (1973): 19–40.
Segall, Shlomi. *Equality and Opportunity*. Oxford: Oxford University Press, 2013.
———. *Health, Luck, and Justice*. Princeton: Princeton University Press, 2009.
Sen, Amartya. *Inequality Reexamined*. New York; Cambridge, MA: Russell Sage Foundation; Harvard University Press, 1992.
Sher, George. *Equality for Inegalitarians*. Cambridge: Cambridge University Press, 2014.
Shields, Liam. *Just Enough: Sufficiency as a Demand of Justice*. Edinburgh: Edinburgh University Press, 2016.
Silvers, Anita. 'No Talent? Beyond the Worst Off! A Diverse Theory of Justice for Disability'. In *Disability and Disadvantage*, edited by Kimberley Brownlee and Adam Cureton, 163–99. Oxford; New York: Oxford University Press, 2009.
Smith, Richard. 'In Search of "Non-disease"'. *BMJ* (Clinical research ed) 324, no. 7342 (Apr. 13, 2002): 883–85.
Solomon, Miriam, Jeremy R. Simon and Harold Kincaid, eds. *The Routledge Companion to Philosophy of Medicine*. London: Routledge, 2017.
Swift, Adam. *Political Philosophy: A Beginners' Guide for Students and Politicians*. Cambridge; Malden, MA: Polity; Blackwell Publishers, 2001.
Thomas, Felicity, and Jasmine Gideon, eds. *Migration, Health and Inequality*. London: Zed Books Ltd., 2013.
Thomson, Garrett. *Needs*. International Library of Philosophy. London; New York: Routledge & Kegan Paul, 1987.
Toombs, S. Kay. *The Meaning of Illness: A Phenomenological Account of the Different Perspectives of Physician and Patient*. Philosophy and Medicine, 42. Dordrecht, Holland; Boston: Kluwer Academic Publishers, 1992.
United Nations General Assembly. *International Covenant on Civil and Political Rights*. United Nations, Human Rights, Office of the High Commissioner. Signed 16 December 1966, New York City. https://www.ohchr.org/EN/ProfessionalInterest/Pages/CCPR.aspx.
———. *Universal Declaration of Human Rights*. Article 25. United Nations (website). Adopted 10 December 1948, Paris. http://www.un.org/en/universal-declaration-human-rights/.
Venkatapuram, Sridhar. *Health Justice: An Argument from the Capabilities Approach*. Cambridge: Polity, 2011.
Walzer, Michael. *Spheres of Justice: A Defense of Pluralism and Equality*. New York: Basic Books, 1983.
Whitehead, Margaret. 'The Concepts and Principles of Equity and Health'. *International Journal of Health Services* 22, no. 3 (1992): 429–45.
Wilkinson, Richard G., and Kate Pickett. *The Spirit Level: Why Greater Equality Makes Societies Stronger*. New York: Bloomsbury Press, 2010.
Wolff, Jonathan. *The Human Right to Health*. Amnesty International Global Ethics Series. New York: W. W. Norton & Co., 2012.

Wolff, Jonathan, and Avner de-Shalit. *Disadvantage*. Oxford Political Theory. Oxford; New York: Oxford University Press, 2007.

World Health Organization. *Constitution of the World Health Organization*. Signed 22 July 1946, New York City. http://apps.who.int/gb/bd/PDF/bd47/EN/constitution-en.pdf.

Young, Iris Marion. *Justice and the Politics of Difference*. Princeton, NJ: Princeton University Press, 1990.

Notes

1. THE CONCEPT OF DISEASE

1. Lawrie Reznek, *The Nature of Disease*, Philosophical Issues in Science (London; New York: Routledge & Kegan Paul, 1987), 171.

2. K. Danner Clouser, Charles M. Culver and Bernard Gert, 'Malady', in *What Is Disease?*, Biomedical Ethics Reviews, ed. James M. Humber and Robert F. Almeder (Totowa, NJ: Humana Press, 1997), 190.

3. 1972, p. 417; English translation courtesy of Daniela Mergenthaler, 'Medicine as Task—Karl E. Rothschuh's Philosophy of Medicine', *Medicine, Health Care and Philosophy* 7, no. 3 (2005): 257.

4. H. Tristram Engelhardt Jr., 'The Concepts of Health and Disease', in *Evaluation and Explanation in the Biomedical Sciences: Proceedings of the First Trans-disciplinary Symposium on Philosophy and Medicine, Held at Galveston, May 9–11, 1974*, Philosophy and Medicine, vol. 1, ed. H. Tristram Engelhardt Jr. and Stuart F. Spicker (Dordrecht, Holland; Boston: Reidel Pub. Co., 1975), 127.

5. Rachel Cooper, 'Disease', *Studies in History and Philosophy of Science Part C: Studies in History and Philosophy of Biological and Biomedical Sciences* 33, no. 2 (2002): 271.

6. Peter Sedgwick, 'Illness: Mental and Otherwise', *The Hastings Center Studies* 1, no. 3, (1973): 30f. Emphasis original.

7. Christopher Boorse, 'Health as a Theoretical Concept', *Philosophy of Science* 44, no. 4 (1977): 567.

2. HEALTH

1. World Health Organization, *Constitution of the World Health Organization*, signed 22 July 1946, New York City, http://apps.who.int/gb/bd/PDF/bd47/EN/constitution-en.pdf.

2. Lennart Nordenfelt, *On the Nature of Health: An Action-Theoretic Approach*, Philosephy and Medicine, vol. 26, 2nd rev. and enl. ed. (Dordrecht, Holland; Boston: Kluwer, 1995), 90.

3. Allen Buchanan, Dan W. Brock, Norman Daniels and Daniel Wikler, *From Chance to Choice: Genetics and Justice* (Cambridge; New York: Cambridge University Press, 2000), 122.

4. Norman Daniels, *Just Health: Meeting Health Needs Fairly* (Cambridge; New York: Cambridge University Press, 2008), 35.

5. D. E. Beauchamp, 'Public Health: III. Philosophy', in *Encyclopedia of Bioethics*, 3rd ed., ed. Stephen G. Post (New York: Macmillan Reference, 1995), 2210.

6. Faculty of Public Health of the Royal College of Physician of the United Kingdom, quoted in Nuffield Council on Bioethics, *Public Health: Ethical Issues* (Cambridge: Cambridge Publishers, 2007), 6.

3. THEORIES OF SOCIAL JUSTICE

1. John Rawls, *A Theory of Justice*, rev. ed. (Cambridge, MA: Belknap Press of Harvard University Press, 1999, first published 1971), 3.

2. David Hume, *Enquiries Concerning Human Understanding and Concerning the Principles of Morals*, 3rd ed., intro., comparative table of contents and analytical index L. A. Selby-Bigge, and text rev. and notes P. H. Nidditch (Oxford: Clarendon Press, 1975), first published 1777. Emphasis original.

3. Michael Walzer, *Spheres of Justice: A Defense of Pluralism and Equality* (New York: Basic Books, 1983).

4. David Miller, *Principles of Social Justice* (Cambridge, MA: Harvard University Press, 1999).

5. Axel Honneth, *Freedom's Right: The Social Foundations of Democratic Life* (Cambridge: Polity Press, 2014).

6. Ronald Dworkin, *Sovereign Virtue: The Theory and Practice of Equality* (Cambridge, MA: Harvard University Press, 2000), 66ff.

7. Rawls, *Theory of Justice*, 47f.

8. Richard B. Brandt, *A Theory of the Good and the Right* (Oxford; New York: Clarendon Press; Oxford University Press, 1979), 20ff.

9. John Rawls, 'The Independence of Moral Theory', *Proceedings and Addresses of the American Philosophical Association* 48 (1974–1975): 8.

10. Norman Daniels, 'Wide Reflective Equilibrium and Theory Acceptance in Ethics', *Journal of Philosophy* 76, no. 5 (1979): 258.

11. John Rawls, *Justice as Fairness: A Restatement*, ed. Erin Kelly (Cambridge, MA: Harvard University Press, 2001), 31.

12. Rawls, 'The Independence of Moral Theory', 8.

13. Amartya Sen, *Inequality Reexamined* (New York; Cambridge, MA: Russell Sage Foundation; Harvard University Press, 1992), 12.

14. Harry Frankfurt, 'Equality as a Moral Ideal', *Ethics* 98, no. 1 (Oct. 1987): 34. *See also* Elizabeth S. Anderson, 'What Is the Point of Equality?' *Ethics* 109, no. 2 (Jan. 1999): 287–337, for a powerful critique of egalitarianism.

15. Robert Nozick, *Anarchy, State, and Utopia* (New York: Basic Books, 1974), 169.

16. Frankfurt, 'Equality as a Moral Ideal', 1987, 21.

17. Joel Feinberg, 'Noncomparative Justice', *The Philosophical Review* 83, no. 3 (1974): 298. Emphasis original.

4. THEORIES OF HEALTH JUSTICE

1. Sen, *Inequality Reexamined*, 40.

2. Madison Powers and Ruth Faden, *Social Justice: The Moral Foundations of Public Health and Health Policy*, Issues in Biomedical Ethics (Oxford; New York: Oxford University Press, 2006), 39.

3. Jennifer Prah Ruger, *Health and Social Justice* (Oxford; New York: Oxford University Press, 2010).
4. Sridhar Venkatapuram, *Health Justice: An Argument from the Capabilities Approach* (Cambridge: Polity, 2011), 71.
5. Norman Daniels, *Just Health Care*, Studies in Philosophy and Health Policy (Cambridge [Cambridgeshire]; New York: Cambridge University Press, 1985).
6. Shlomi Segall, *Equality and Opportunity* (Oxford: Oxford University Press, 2013), 177.
7. Talcott Parsons, 'The Sick Role and the Role of the Physician Reconsidered', *Milbank Memorial Fund Quarterly: Health and Society* 53, no. 3 (Feb. 1975): 267.

5. GLOBAL HEALTH JUSTICE

1. United Nations General Assembly, *Universal Declaration of Human Rights*, article 25, United Nations (website), adopted 10 December 1948, Paris, http://www.un.org/en/universal-declaration-human-rights/.
2. Preamble to World Health Organization, *Constitution of the World Health Organization.*
3. Ibid.
4. United Nations General Assembly, *International Covenant on Civil and Political Rights*, United Nations, Human Rights, Office of the High Commissioner, signed 16 December 1966, New York City, https://www.ohchr.org/EN/ProfessionalInterest/Pages/CCPR.aspx.
5. World Health Organization. http://who.int/gho/mortality_burden_disease/life_tables/situation_trends/en/.
6. Ibid.
7. Margaret Whitehead, 'The Concepts and Principles of Equity and Health'. *International Journal of Health Services* 22, no. 3 (1992): 429–45.

6. CURTAILING HEALTH PROMOTION

1. Richard Smith, 'In Search of "Non-disease"', *BMJ* (Clinical research ed.) 324, no. 7342 (Apr. 13, 2002): 885.
2. Peter Conrad, 'Medicalization and Social Control', *Annual Review of Sociology* 18 (1992): 223.
3. Edmund D. Pellegrino, 'The Goals and Ends of Medicine: How Are They to Be Defined?' in *The Goals of Medicine: The Forgotten Issue in Health Care Reform*, ed. Mark J. Hanson and Daniel Callahan, Hastings Center Studies in Ethics (Washington, DC: Georgetown University Press, 1999), 62.
4. Leon Kass, *Toward a More Natural Science: Biology and Human Affairs* (New York: Free Press, 1985), 159.
5. Mark J. Hanson and Daniel Callahan, eds., *The Goals of Medicine: The Forgotten Issue in Health Care Reform*, Hastings Center Studies in Ethics (Washington, DC: Georgetown University Press, 1999).
6. Ibid., S6.

7. A SUFFICIENTARIAN THEORY OF HEALTH JUSTICE

1. John Harris, 'Is There a Coherent Social Conception of Disability?' *J Med Ethics* 26, no. 2 (Apr. 2000), https://jme.bmj.com/content/26/2/95, 98.

2. H. Tristram Engelhardt Jr., *The Foundations of Bioethics*, 2nd ed. (New York: Oxford University Press, 1996) 197.

3. Found in Roger Ebert, 'Sundance #3: Of Heart and Humor', Festivals & Awards, Roger-Ebert.com, 7 August 2005, http://rogerebert.suntimes.com/apps/pbcs.dll/article?AID=/20050125/FILMFESTIVALS05/501250301/1023.

4. Seth Farber, *Madness, Heresy, and the Rumor of Angels: The Revolt against the Mental Health System* (Chicago: Open Court, 1993), 95.

5. Segall, *Equality and Opportunity*, 42.

6. Anita Silvers, 'No Talent? Beyond the Worst Off! A Diverse Theory of Justice for Disability', in *Disability and Disadvantage*, ed. Kimberley Brownlee and Adam Cureton (Oxford; New York: Oxford University Press, 2009), 180.

7. Ibid., 180f.

8. Ibid., 181.

9. Jonathan Wolff and Avner De-Shalit, *Disadvantage*, Oxford Political Theory (Oxford; New York: Oxford University Press, 2007), 9.

10. T. H. Marshall, *Citizenship and Social Class, and Other Essays* (Cambridge: Cambridge University Press, 1950).

11. Garrett Thomson, *Needs*, International Library of Philosophy (London; New York: Routledge & Kegan Paul, 1987), 3.

Index

About the Author

Thomas Schramme is Professor of Philosophy at the University of Liverpool. He has published widely in philosophy of medicine, including the *Handbook of the Philosophy of Medicine* (co-edited with Steven Edwards; 2017), *New Perspectives on Paternalism and Health Care* (2015) and *Being Amoral: Psychopathy and Moral Incapacity* (2014).

www.ingramcontent.com/pod-product-compliance
Ingram Content Group UK Ltd.
Pitfield, Milton Keynes, MK11 3LW, UK
UKHW012042150926
475560UK00001B/136

9 781786 60143